cupcakes

METRO BOOKS
New York

An Imprint of Sterling Publishing
387 Park Avenue South
New York, NY 10016

ISBN 978-1-4351-4237-4

cupcakes

Pamela Clark

METRO BOOKS
New York

contents

introduction

These exquisite little cakes are ideal for afternoon tea, as an elegant and chic dessert for a dinner party, or as a splendid and original birthday cake. While it's true they look like little works of art, and a few of them require some cake decorating experience, most of them are not difficult to make. My team and I have had the best fun dreaming up ideas for the design of these little masterpieces, and playing with the flavors so they complement the look of the cakes.

veryberry cakes

You can make vanilla sugar by adding one whole vanilla bean to a jar of granulated sugar. The sugar will keep indefinitely.

Dried berry buttercake

1 stick butter, softened
½ teaspoon vanilla extract
⅔ cup sugar
2 eggs
1 cup dried mixed berries
½ cup slivered almonds
⅔ cup all-purpose flour
⅓ cup self-rising flour
¼ cup milk

Sugared fruit

5 ounces fresh blueberries
4 ounces fresh raspberries
1 egg white, beaten lightly
3 tablespoons vanilla sugar

Cream cheese frosting

2 tablespoons butter, softened
3 ounces cream cheese, softened
1½ cups powdered sugar

1 Prepare sugared fruit.
2 Preheat oven to 325°F. Line 6-hole oversize (Texas) or 12-hole standard muffin pan with paper baking cups.
3 Beat butter, vanilla, sugar and eggs in small bowl with electric mixer until light and fluffy. Stir in fruit and nuts, then sifted flours and milk. Divide mixture among baking cups; smooth surface.
4 Bake large cakes about 45 minutes, small cakes about 35 minutes. Turn cakes onto wire rack to cool.
5 Make cream cheese frosting.
6 Spread cakes with frosting. Decorate with sugared fruit.

Sugared fruit

Brush each berry lightly with egg white; roll fruit in sugar. Place fruit on parchment paper-lined tray. Leave about 1 hour or until sugar is dry.

Cream cheese frosting

Beat butter and cheese in small bowl with electric mixer until light and fluffy; gradually beat in sifted powdered sugar.

pear butterfly cakes

Pear and maple buttercake
1 medium fresh pear (8 ounces),
   grated coarsely
5 tablespoons butter, softened
¼ cup self-rising flour
¾ cup all-purpose flour
1 teaspoon ground cinnamon
½ cup firmly packed
   brown sugar
¼ cup maple-flavored syrup
2 eggs
⅓ cup coarsely chopped pecans
⅓ cup finely chopped dried pear

Pear butterflies
1½ tablespoons sugar
1½ tablespoons water
1 medium brown pear (8 ounces)
   (eg Beurre bosc), sliced thinly

Fondant icing
1 pound white prepared fondant,
   chopped coarsely
1 egg white
blue, pink and yellow
   food coloring

1 Make pear butterflies.
2 Preheat oven to 350°F.
Line 6-hole oversize (Texas) or
12-hole standard muffin pan
with paper baking cups.
3 Drain fresh pear, squeezing
out as much juice as possible.
You need ⅔ cup grated pear.
4 Beat butter, flours, cinnamon,
sugar, syrup and eggs in small
bowl with electric mixer on low
speed until ingredients are
combined. Beat on medium
speed until mixture is changed
to a paler color.
5 Stir in fresh pear, nuts and
dried pear. Divide mixture among
baking cups; smooth surface.
6 Bake large cakes about
35 minutes, small cakes about
30 minutes. Turn cakes onto
wire rack to cool.
7 Make fondant icing. Divide
icing into three small bowls;
using colorings, tint icing pale
blue, pink and yellow. Spoon
icing quickly over cakes, level
with tops of baking cups; allow
to set.
8 Top cakes with pear slices.

Pear butterflies
Preheat oven to 250°F. Combine
sugar and the water in small
pot. Stir over medium heat,
without boiling, until sugar is
dissolved. Bring to a boil, reduce
heat; simmer, without stirring,
1 minute. Brush pear slices on
both sides with sugar syrup.
Place slices in a single layer on
a wire rack over baking sheet
(see page 125). Dry in oven
about 40 minutes. While pears
are still warm, shape into
butterfly wings (see page 125).
Cool on wire rack.

Fondant icing
Place fondant in a medium
bowl over a medium pot of
simmering water; stir until
smooth. Stir in egg white. Let
stand at room temperature
for about 10 minutes or until
thickened slightly.

Chocolate ginger cake

½ cup firmly packed
  brown sugar
½ cup all-purpose flour
½ cup self-rising flour
¼ teaspoon baking soda
1 teaspoon ground ginger
½ teaspoon ground cinnamon
¼ teaspoon ground nutmeg
6 tablespoons butter, softened
1 egg
¼ cup buttermilk
3 tablespoons honey
2 ounces dark chocolate,
  chopped coarsely

Decorations

1½ cups heavy cream
6 ounces chocolate-covered
  toffee bars (such as Skor or
  Heath), chopped coarsely

1 Preheat oven to 325°F.
Line 6-hole oversize (Texas) or
12-hole standard muffin pan
with paper baking cups.

2 Sift dry ingredients into small
bowl, add butter, egg, buttermilk
and syrup; beat mixture with
electric mixer on low speed
until ingredients are combined.
Increase speed to medium,
beat until mixture is changed to
a paler color. Stir in chocolate.
Divide mixture among baking
cups; smooth surface.

3 Bake large cakes about
40 minutes, small cakes about
30 minutes. Turn cakes onto
wire rack to cool.

4 Spread cakes with whipped
cream; top with toffee bars.

toffee creams

Vanilla buttercake

6 tablespoons butter, softened
½ teaspoon vanilla extract
½ cup sugar
2 eggs
1 cup self-rising flour
3 tablespoons milk

Butter cream frosting

1 stick butter, softened
1½ cups powdered sugar
3 tablespoons milk
2 ounces dark chocolate,
   chopped finely
1½ tablespoons cocoa powder
pink food coloring

Decorations

ice cream waffle cones
strawberry slices
toasted flaked coconut
finely grated dark chocolate

1 Preheat oven to 350°F. Line 6-hole oversize (Texas) or 12-hole standard muffin pan with paper baking cups.
2 Beat butter, vanilla, sugar, eggs, flour and milk in small bowl with electric mixer on low speed until ingredients are just combined. Increase speed to medium, beat until mixture is changed to a paler color.
3 Divide mixture among baking cups; smooth surface.
4 Bake large cakes about 25 minutes, small cakes about 20 minutes. Turn cakes onto wire rack to cool.
5 Make butter cream frosting.
6 Remove baking cups from cakes. Using a serrated knife, shape cakes into balls (see page 124) so they sit inside waffle cones.
7 Place cakes in cones, spread with frosting; decorate with strawberries, toasted coconut and grated chocolate.

Butter cream frosting

Beat butter in small bowl with electric mixer until light and fluffy; beat in sifted powdered sugar and milk, in two batches. Divide mixture among four small bowls. Add chopped chocolate to one and sifted cocoa to another. Using coloring, tint one pink and leave one plain.

ice-cream cone cakes

A pavlova is a delicious Australian meringue dessert, which is baked slowly in the oven so that the outside becomes crunchy while the inside stays chewy.

Cream cheese lemon cake

6 tablespoons butter, softened
3 ounces cream cheese, softened
2 teaspoons finely grated lemon peel
⅔ cup sugar
2 eggs
⅓ cup self-rising flour
½ cup all-purpose flour

Meringue baking cups

3 egg whites
¾ cup sugar
1½ tablespoons cornstarch
1 teaspoon white vinegar
½ teaspoon vanilla extract

Decorations

1½ cups heavy cream, whipped
4 ounces strawberries, quartered
1½ tablespoons passion fruit pulp
½ cup blueberries
1 medium banana (8 ounces), sliced thickly

1 Make meringue baking cups.
2 Preheat oven to 350°F. Line 6-hole oversize (Texas) or 12-hole standard muffin pan with paper baking cups.
3 Beat butter, cheese, lemon peel, sugar and eggs in small bowl with electric mixer until light and fluffy.
4 Add flours to cheese mixture; beat on low speed until combined. Divide mixture among baking cups; smooth surface.
5 Bake large cakes about 30 minutes, small cakes about 20 minutes. Turn cakes onto wire rack to cool.
6 Drop a teaspoon of whipped cream on each cake; top with meringue baking cups. Spoon remaining cream into baking cups and decorate with fruit.

Meringue baking cups

Preheat oven to 250°F. Grease baking sheet; line with parchment paper, trace six 3-inch circles onto paper for large cakes, and twelve 2-inch circles for small cakes. Beat egg whites in small bowl with electric mixer until soft peaks form. Gradually add sugar, a tablespoon at a time, beating until sugar dissolves between additions. Fold in cornstarch, vinegar and vanilla. Spoon meringue inside circles on baking sheet; hollow out slightly. Bake 45 minutes or until baking cups are firm. Cool in oven with door ajar.

lemon pavlova puffs

choc-mint mousse cakes

You can make your own almond meal by grinding blanched almonds in a nut mill or food processor until they reach the consistency of cornmeal.

Double chocolate mint cake

4 ounces square after-dinner mints
2 ounces dark chocolate, chopped coarsely
⅔ cup water
6 tablespoons butter, softened
½ teaspoon peppermint extract
1 cup firmly packed brown sugar
2 eggs
⅔ cup self-rising flour
3 tablespoons cocoa powder
⅓ cup almond meal
1½ tablespoons cocoa powder, extra

Chocolate mousse

5 ounces dark chocolate, chopped roughly
½ teaspoon peppermint extract
¾ cup heavy cream
2 eggs, separated
3 tablespoons sugar

1 Make chocolate mousse.
2 Preheat oven to 325°F. Line 6-hole oversize (Texas) or 12-hole standard muffin pan with paper baking cups.
3 For large cakes, using a 1½-inch long petal cutter, cut out petals from after-dinner mints. For small cakes use a ½-inch long petal cutter to cut petals from after-dinner mints. Coarsely chop remaining mint pieces; reserve for cake mixture.
4 Combine chocolate and the water in small pot; stir over low heat until smooth.
5 Beat butter, extract, sugar and eggs in small bowl with electric mixer until light and fluffy.
6 Stir in sifted flour and cocoa, almond meal, warm chocolate mixture and reserved after-dinner mints. Divide mixture among baking cups; smooth surface.
7 Bake large cakes about 40 minutes, small cakes about 30 minutes. Turn cakes onto wire rack to cool.

8 Place a lightly greased collar of foil around each cake. Divide firm chocolate mousse evenly among tops of cakes. Freeze cakes for about 30 minutes to help set the mousse quickly.
9 Dust mousse with extra sifted cocoa; arrange petals on top in a flower. Gently remove foil; dip spatula in hot water and smooth sides of mousse.

Chocolate mousse

Combine chocolate, extract and half the cream in a medium heatproof bowl over a medium pot of simmering water; stir until smooth. Cool mixture 5 minutes, then stir in egg yolks. Beat remaining cream in small bowl with electric mixer until soft peaks form. Beat egg whites in another small bowl with electric mixer until soft peaks form; add sugar gradually, beat until dissolved. Fold cream into chocolate mixture, then egg whites. Spoon mixture into a shallow baking dish. Cover; refrigerate 4 hours or until firm.

sugar & lace

Caramel mud cake

1 stick butter, chopped coarsely
3½ ounces white chocolate,
    chopped coarsely
⅔ cup firmly packed brown sugar
¼ cup honey
⅔ cup milk
1 cup all-purpose flour
⅓ cup self-rising flour
1 egg

Decorations

doily, lace or stencil
½ cup powdered sugar

1 Preheat oven to 325°F. Line 6-hole oversize (Texas) or 12-hole standard muffin pan with paper baking cups.
2 Combine butter, chocolate, sugar, syrup and milk in small pot; stir over low heat, until smooth. Transfer mixture to medium bowl; cool 15 minutes.
3 Whisk sifted flours into chocolate mixture, then egg. Divide among baking cups.
4 Bake large cakes about 40 minutes, small cakes about 30 minutes. Turn cakes onto wire rack to cool.
5 Place doily, lace or stencil over cake; sift a little powdered sugar over doily (see page 124), then carefully lift doily from cake. Repeat with remaining cakes and powdered sugar.

cloud cakes

Strawberry swirl buttercake
6 tablespoons butter, softened
½ teaspoon vanilla extract
½ cup sugar
2 eggs
1 cup self-rising flour
3 tablespoons milk
3 tablespoons strawberry jam

Fluffy frosting
1 cup sugar
⅓ cup water
2 egg whites

Decorations
pink colored sugar
  (see page 125)

1 Preheat oven to 350°F.
Line 6-hole oversize (Texas) or
12-hole standard muffin pan
with paper baking cups.
2 Beat butter, vanilla, sugar,
eggs, flour and milk in small
bowl with electric mixer on low
speed until ingredients are just
combined. Increase speed to
medium, beat until mixture is
changed to a paler color.
3 Divide mixture among baking
cups; smooth surface. Divide
jam over tops of cakes; using a
skewer, swirl jam into cakes.
4 Bake large cakes about
30 minutes, small cakes about
20 minutes. Turn cakes onto
wire rack to cool.
5 Make fluffy frosting.
6 Spread cakes with frosting;
sprinkle with colored sugar.

Fluffy frosting
Combine sugar and the water
in small pot; stir over medium
heat, without boiling, until sugar
is dissolved. Boil, uncovered,
without stirring about 5 minutes
or until syrup reaches 240°F on
a candy thermometer. Syrup
should be thick but not colored.
Remove from heat, allow
bubbles to subside. Beat egg
whites in small bowl with electric
mixer until soft peaks form.
While mixer is running, add hot
syrup in thin stream; beat on
high speed about 10 minutes or
until mixture is thick and cool.

23

toffee-apple towers

Maple, pecan and apple cake

5 tablespoons butter, softened
1 cup self-rising flour
1 teaspoon ground cinnamon
½ cup firmly packed
  brown sugar
¼ cup maple-flavored syrup
2 eggs
⅔ cup coarsely chopped pecans
½ cup coarsely grated apple

Maple frosting

6 tablespoons butter, softened
1 cup powdered sugar
2 teaspoons maple-flavored syrup

Toffee

1 cup sugar
½ cup water

1 Preheat oven to 350°F.
Line 6-hole oversize (Texas) or
12-hole standard muffin pan
with paper baking cups.
2 Beat butter, flour, cinnamon,
sugar, syrup and eggs in small
bowl with electric mixer on low
speed until ingredients are
combined. Increase speed to
medium, beat until mixture is
changed to a paler color.
3 Stir in nuts and grated apple.
Divide mixture among baking
cups; smooth surface.
4 Bake large cakes about
35 minutes, small cakes about
25 minutes. Turn cakes onto
wire rack to cool.
5 Make maple frosting.
Make toffee.
6 Spread cakes with frosting;
decorate with toffee shards.

Maple frosting

Beat butter, sifted powdered
sugar and syrup in small bowl
with electric mixer until light
and fluffy.

Toffee

Combine sugar with the water
in small heavy-based pot. Stir
over medium heat, without
boiling, until sugar dissolves;
bring to a boil. Reduce heat;
simmer, uncovered, without
stirring, until mixture is golden
brown. Remove from heat; let
stand until bubbles subside.
Make toffee shards on
parchment paper-lined baking
sheet (see page 119).

turkish delights

You can buy both Turkish delight and rosewater at Mediterranean or Middle Eastern markets, or at some gourmet grocery stores.

White chocolate pistachio cake
2 ounces white chocolate, chopped roughly
3 tablespoons rose water
½ cup water
⅓ cup pistachio nuts
6 tablespoons butter, softened
1 cup firmly packed brown sugar
2 eggs
⅔ cup self-rising flour
3 tablespoons all-purpose flour

Decorations
⅔ cup coarsely chopped pistachio nuts
10½ ounces white chocolate, melted
2 pounds Turkish delight, chopped

1 Preheat oven to 350°F. Line 6-hole oversize (Texas) or 12-hole standard muffin pan with paper baking cups.
2 Combine chocolate, rose water and the water in small pot; stir over low heat until smooth.
3 Blend or process nuts until fine.
4 Beat butter, sugar and eggs in small bowl with electric mixer until combined.
5 Fold in sifted flours, ground pistachios and warm chocolate mixture. Divide mixture among baking cups.
6 Bake large cakes about 35 minutes, small cakes about 25 minutes. Turn cakes onto wire rack to cool.
7 Cut a 1¼-inch deep hole in the center of each cake; fill with a few chopped nuts. Drizzle with a little chocolate; replace lids.
8 Decorate cakes with pieces of Turkish delight and chopped nuts dipped in chocolate.

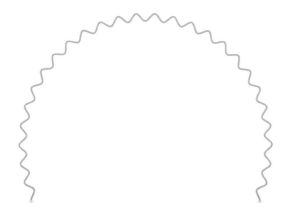

rocky road cakes

Marble cake

1 stick butter, softened
½ teaspoon vanilla extract
⅔ cup sugar
2 eggs
1¼ cups self-rising flour
⅓ cup milk
pink food coloring
1½ tablespoons cocoa powder
2 teaspoons milk, extra

Rocky road topping

½ cup unsalted roasted peanuts
1 cup red candied cherries, halved
1 cup pink and white
    marshmallows,
    chopped coarsely
½ cup flaked coconut, toasted
7 ounces milk chocolate, melted

Decorations

2 ounces milk chocolate chips,
    melted

1 Preheat oven to 350°F. Line 6-hole oversize (Texas) or 12-hole standard muffin pan with paper baking cups.

2 Beat butter, vanilla, sugar and eggs in small bowl with electric mixer until light and fluffy. Stir in sifted flour and milk in two batches.

3 Divide mixture evenly among three bowls. Tint one mixture pink. Blend sifted cocoa with extra milk in cup; stir into another mixture. Leave third mixture plain.

4 Drop alternate spoonfuls of the mixtures into baking cups. Pull a skewer backwards and forwards through mixtures for a marbled effect; smooth surface.

5 Bake large cakes about 30 minutes, small cakes about 20 minutes. Turn cakes onto wire rack to cool.

6 Combine ingredients for rocky road topping in medium bowl.

7 Place topping on tops of cakes; drizzle with chocolate.

angel cakes

Vanilla buttercake

6 tablespoons butter, softened
½ teaspoon vanilla extract
½ cup sugar
2 eggs
1 cup self-rising flour
3 tablespoons milk

Chocolate icing

¾ tablespoon butter
⅓ cup milk
2 cups powdered sugar
¼ cup cocoa powder

Decorations

1 cup unsweetened
  shredded coconut
¼ cup raspberry jam
½ cup heavy cream, whipped

1 Preheat oven to 350°F. Line 6-hole oversize (Texas) or 12-hole standard muffin pan with paper baking cups.
2 Beat butter, vanilla, sugar, eggs, flour and milk in small bowl with electric mixer on low speed until ingredients are just combined. Increase speed to medium, beat until mixture is changed to a paler color.
3 Divide mixture among baking cups; smooth surface.
4 Bake large cakes about 25 minutes, small cakes about 20 minutes. Turn cakes onto wire rack to cool.
5 Make chocolate icing.
6 Remove baking cups from cakes. Dip cakes in icing; drain off excess, toss cakes in coconut. Place cakes on wire rack to set.
7 Cut cakes as desired; fill with jam and cream.

Chocolate icing

Melt butter in medium heatproof bowl over medium pot of simmering water. Stir in milk and sifted powdered sugar and cocoa until icing is of a coating consistency.

Ginger buttermilk cake

½ cup firmly packed
   brown sugar
½ cup all-purpose flour
½ cup self-rising flour
¼ teaspoon baking soda
1 teaspoon ground ginger
½ teaspoon ground cinnamon
¼ teaspoon ground nutmeg
6 tablespoons butter, softened
1 egg
¼ cup buttermilk
3 tablespoons honey

Decorations

½ cup powdered sugar
14 ounces white prepared
   fondant
⅓ cup ginger marmalade,
   warmed, strained
2 ounces red prepared fondant
2 ounces black prepared fondant

1 Preheat oven to 325°F.
Line 6-hole oversize (Texas) or
12-hole standard muffin pan
with paper baking cups.
2 Sift dry ingredients into
small bowl, then add remaining
ingredients. Beat mixture with
electric mixer on low speed
until ingredients are combined.
Increase speed to medium,
beat until mixture is changed
to a paler color.
3 Divide mixture among baking
cups; smooth surface.
4 Bake large cakes about
40 minutes, small cakes about
30 minutes. Turn cakes onto
wire rack to cool.
5 Dust surface with sifted
powdered sugar; knead white
prepared fondant until smooth.
Roll out fondant to a thickness
of ¼ inch. Cut out rounds large
enough to cover tops of cakes.

6 Brush tops of cakes with
marmalade; cover with fondant
rounds (see page 120).
7 Roll out red and black
fondants, separately, until
¼-inch thick. Cut out shapes
using heart, diamond, club and
spade cutters (see page 115).
8 Roll out red and black fondant
scraps, separately, to a thickness
of ⅛ inch. Cut out 'A's using an
alphabet cutter set (see page 115).
9 Secure fondant shapes to
cakes by brushing backs with a
tiny amount of water.

sweet ginger aces

coconut kisses

Only slightly less common than Ferrero Rocher, these coconut-covered wafers enclose a creamy filling and a whole almond.

White chocolate mud cake
1 stick butter, chopped coarsely
3 ounces white chocolate, chopped coarsely
1 cup sugar
½ cup milk
½ cup all-purpose flour
½ cup self-rising flour
½ teaspoon coconut extract
1 egg

Whipped white chocolate ganache
¼ cup cream
6½ ounces white chocolate, chopped coarsely
1½ tablespoons coconut liqueur

Decorations
three 5-ounce boxes ferrero raffaelo chocolate truffles

1 Preheat oven to 325°F. Line 6-hole oversize (Texas) or 12-hole standard muffin pan with paper baking cups.
2 Combine butter, chocolate, sugar and milk in small pot; stir over low heat until smooth. Transfer mixture to medium bowl; cool 15 minutes.
3 Whisk in sifted flours, then coconut extract and egg. Divide mixture among baking cups; smooth surface.
4 Bake large cakes about 40 minutes, small cakes about 30 minutes. Turn cakes onto wire rack to cool.
5 Make whipped white chocolate ganache.
6 Spread cakes with ganache. Top with halved truffles, then stack with whole truffles using a little ganache to secure.

Whipped white chocolate ganache
Bring cream to a boil in small pot; pour over chocolate and liqueur in small bowl of electric mixer, stir until smooth. Cover; refrigerate 30 minutes. Beat with an electric mixer until light and fluffy.

froufrou

Raspberry coconut cake

1 stick butter, softened
1 cup sugar
3 eggs
½ cup all-purpose flour
¼ cup self-rising flour
½ cup unsweetened
    shredded coconut
⅓ cup sour cream
5 ounces frozen raspberries

Cream cheese frosting

5 tablespoons butter, softened
12 ounces cream cheese,
    softened
2 teaspoons coconut extract
3 cups powdered sugar

Decorations

1 cup flaked coconut, toasted
15 fresh raspberries, halved

1 Preheat oven to 350°F.
Line 6-hole oversize (Texas) or
12-hole standard muffin pan
with paper baking cups.
2 Beat butter, sugar and eggs
in small bowl with electric mixer
until light and fluffy.
3 Stir in sifted flours, coconut,
sour cream and frozen raspberries.
Divide mixture among baking
cups; smooth surface.
4 Bake large cakes about
50 minutes, small cakes about
40 minutes. Turn cakes onto
wire rack to cool.
5 Make cream cheese frosting.
6 Remove baking cups from
cakes; spread cakes with frosting.
7 Decorate cakes with coconut
and raspberries.

Cream cheese frosting

Beat butter, cream cheese and
coconut extract in small bowl
with electric mixer until light and
fluffy; gradually beat in sifted
powdered sugar.

mochaccinos

You will need six 12-ounce or twelve 4-ounce capacity coffee cups for this recipe.

Mocha mud cake

1 stick plus 3 tablespoons
butter, chopped coarsely
3½ ounces dark chocolate,
chopped coarsely
1⅓ cups sugar
⅔ cup water
¼ cup coffee liqueur
3 tablespoons instant
coffee granules
1 cup all-purpose flour
3 tablespoons self-rising flour
3 tablespoons cocoa powder
1 egg

Decorations

1½ cups heavy cream, whipped
3 tablespoons chocolate syrup
1½ tablespoons cocoa powder

1 Preheat oven to 325°F.
Line 6-hole oversize (Texas) or
12-hole standard muffin pan
with paper baking cups.
2 Combine butter, chocolate,
sugar, the water, liqueur and
coffee in small pot; stir over
low heat until smooth.
3 Transfer mixture to medium
bowl; cool 15 minutes. Whisk
in sifted flours and cocoa, then
egg. Divide mixture among
baking cups.
4 Bake large cakes about
1 hour, small cakes about
50 minutes. Turn cakes onto
wire rack to cool.
5 Remove baking cups from
cakes. Place cakes in coffee
cups, top with cream. Place
chocolate syrup into piping
bag fitted with small plain tube,
pipe spirals over cream; feather
and fan cakes by pulling a
skewer through the spirals
(see page 124) or, dust cakes
with sifted cocoa.

life's a beach at 30

We used scrap-booking decorations available from craft and hobby shops. This cake can be assembled directly onto a table or covered 24-inch square cake plate.

Lime coconut cake

2 sticks butter, softened
2 teaspoons coconut extract
1½ tablespoons finely grated lime peel
1⅓ cups sugar
4 eggs
⅔ cup milk
1½ cups unsweetened shredded coconut
2½ cups self-rising flour

Coconut cream cheese frosting

5 tablespoons butter, softened
5 ounces cream cheese, softened
2 teaspoons coconut extract
3 cups (1 pound) powdered sugar

Decorations

2 ounces vanilla wafers, crushed finely
beach-themed decorations

1 Preheat oven to 350°F. Line two 12-hole standard muffin pans with paper baking cups.
2 Beat butter, coconut extract, lime peel, sugar and eggs in large bowl with electric mixer until combined.
3 Stir in milk and coconut, then sifted flour. Divide mixture among baking cups; smooth surface.
4 Bake cakes about 25 minutes. Turn cakes onto wire rack to cool.
5 Make coconut cream cheese frosting.
6 Cover backs of decorations with parchment paper to prevent staining.
7 Spread cakes with frosting; dip tops of cakes into vanilla wafer crumbs, top with decorations.

Coconut cream cheese frosting

Beat butter, cream cheese and coconut extract in small bowl with electric mixer until light and fluffy; gradually beat in sifted powdered sugar.

You can make your own almond meal by grinding blanched almonds in a nut mill or food processor until they reach the consistency of cornmeal.

Double chocolate mud cake

2 ounces dark chocolate, chopped coarsely
⅔ cup water
6 tablespoons butter, softened
1 cup firmly packed brown sugar
2 eggs
⅔ cup self-rising flour
3 tablespoons cocoa powder
⅓ cup almond meal

Milk chocolate ganache

3½ ounces milk chocolate, chopped coarsely
¼ cup cream

Florentine topping

1 cup sliced almonds, toasted
½ cup coarsely chopped candied ginger
1 cup red candied cherries, halved

Decorations

2 ounces dark chocolate, melted

1 Preheat oven to 325°F. Line 6-hole oversize (Texas) or 12-hole standard muffin pan with paper baking cups.
2 Combine chocolate and the water in small pot; stir over low heat until smooth.
3 Beat butter, sugar and eggs in small bowl with electric mixer until light and fluffy.
4 Stir in sifted flour and cocoa, almond meal and warm chocolate mixture. Divide mixture among baking cups; smooth surface.
5 Bake large cakes about 35 minutes, small cakes about 25 minutes. Turn cakes onto wire rack to cool.
6 Make milk chocolate ganache.
7 Combine ingredients for florentine topping in small bowl.
8 Spread cakes with ganache, top with florentine mixture; drizzle with chocolate.

Milk chocolate ganache

Bring cream to a boil in small pot, pour over chocolate in small bowl; stir until smooth. Let stand at room temperature until ganache is spreadable.

baby blue

You can make your own almond meal by grinding blanched almonds in a nut mill or food processor until they reach the consistency of cornmeal.

Choc-orange almond cake

2 ounces dark chocolate, chopped coarsely
1 teaspoon finely grated orange peel
⅔ cup orange juice
6 tablespoons butter, softened
1 cup firmly packed brown sugar
2 eggs
⅔ cup self-rising flour
3 tablespoons cocoa powder
⅓ cup almond meal

Decorations

½ cup powdered sugar
14 ounces white prepared fondant
blue food coloring
⅓ cup orange marmalade, warmed, strained
2 yards ribbon, approximately

1 Preheat oven to 325°F. Line 6-hole oversize (Texas) or 12-hole standard muffin pan with paper baking cups.
2 Combine chocolate, orange peel and orange juice in small pot; stir over low heat until smooth.
3 Beat butter, sugar and eggs in small bowl with electric mixer until light and fluffy.
4 Stir in sifted flour and cocoa, almond meal and warm chocolate mixture. Divide mixture among baking cups; smooth surface.
5 Bake large cakes about 35 minutes, small cakes about 25 minutes. Turn cakes onto wire rack to cool.
6 Dust surface with sifted powdered sugar, knead fondant until smooth. Knead blue coloring into fondant (see page 120).
7 Brush tops of cakes with marmalade. Roll fondant out to ¼-inch thickness; cut rounds large enough to cover tops of cakes.
8 Place rounds on cakes; tie cakes with ribbon.

tiramisu

Vanilla buttercake

6 tablespoons butter, softened
½ teaspoon vanilla extract
½ cup sugar
2 eggs
1 cup self-rising flour
3 tablespoons milk

Mascarpone cream

8 ounces mascarpone cheese
¼ cup powdered sugar
1½ tablespoons marsala
¾ cup heavy cream, whipped

Coffee mixture

1½ tablespoons instant
   coffee granules
⅓ cup boiling water
3 tablespoons marsala

Decorations

2 ounces dark chocolate,
   grated finely

1 Preheat oven to 350°F.
Line 6-hole oversize (Texas) or
12-hole standard muffin pan
with paper baking cups.
2 Beat butter, vanilla, sugar,
eggs, flour and milk in small
bowl with electric mixer on low
speed until ingredients are just
combined. Increase speed to
medium, beat until mixture is
changed to a paler color. Divide
mixture among baking cups;
smooth surface.
3 Bake large cakes about
25 minutes, small cakes about
20 minutes. Turn cakes onto
wire rack to cool.
4 Make mascarpone cream.
Make coffee mixture.
5 Remove baking cups from
cakes. Cut each cake horizontally
into four. Brush both sides of cake
slices with coffee mixture. Join cake
slices with mascarpone cream.
6 Spread tops of cakes with
mascarpone cream; sprinkle with
grated chocolate. Refrigerate for
3 hours before serving.

Mascarpone cream

Combine mascarpone, sifted
powdered sugar and marsala in
small bowl; fold in cream.

Coffee mixture

Combine coffee, the water and
marsala in small bowl; cool.

lemon cheesecakes

Lemon cheesecake

3½ ounces vanilla wafers
4 tablespoons butter, melted
two 8-ounce packages cream
  cheese, softened
2 teaspoons finely grated
  lemon peel
½ cup sugar
2 eggs

Glaze

⅔ cup apricot jam
3 tablespoons brandy

1 Preheat oven to 275°F.
Line 6-hole oversize (Texas) or
12-hole standard muffin pan
with paper baking cups.
2 Blend or process cookies until
fine. Add butter; process until
just combined. Divide mixture
among baking cups; press firmly.
Refrigerate 30 minutes.
3 Beat cheese, lemon peel and
sugar in small bowl with electric
mixer until smooth. Beat in eggs.
Pour mixture into baking cups.
4 Bake large cakes about
30 minutes, small cakes about
25 minutes. Cool.
5 Make glaze.
6 Pour glaze evenly over tops of
cheesecakes; refrigerate 2 hours
or until glaze is set.

Glaze

Heat jam and brandy in small
pot over low heat; strain.

Fig, caramel and walnut cake

1 stick butter, softened
½ teaspoon vanilla extract
⅔ cup sugar
2 eggs
¾ cup finely chopped dried figs
½ cup finely chopped walnuts
⅔ cup all-purpose flour
⅓ cup self-rising flour
2-ounce mars bar, chopped finely
¼ cup milk

Whipped milk chocolate ganache

⅓ cup cream
7 ounces milk chocolate

Toffee

½ cup sugar
¼ cup water

Decorations

6 medium fresh figs (12 ounces), quartered

1 Preheat oven to 350°F. Line 6-hole oversize (Texas) or 12-hole standard muffin pan with paper baking cups.

2 Beat butter, vanilla, sugar and eggs in small bowl with electric mixer until light and fluffy.

3 Stir in figs, nuts, sifted flours, mars bar and milk. Divide mixture among baking cups; smooth surface.

4 Bake large cakes about 40 minutes, small cakes about 30 minutes. Turn cakes onto wire rack to cool.

5 Make whipped milk chocolate ganache.

6 Make toffee; form into shapes over rolling pin (see page 119).

7 Spread cakes with ganache; decorate with fig quarters and toffee shapes.

Whipped milk chocolate ganache

Bring cream to a boil in small pot, pour over chocolate in small bowl of electric mixer, stir until smooth. Cover; refrigerate for 30 minutes. Beat with electric mixer until light and fluffy.

Toffee

Combine sugar with the water in small heavy-based pot. Stir over medium heat, without boiling, until sugar dissolves; bring to a boil. Reduce heat; simmer, uncovered, without stirring, until mixture is golden brown. Remove from heat; let stand until bubbles subside.

fig and toffee crowns

You can make your own almond meal by grinding blanched almonds in a nut mill or food processor until they reach the consistency of cornmeal.

orange blossom cakes

Orange, almond and craisin cake

1 stick butter, softened
2 teaspoons finely grated orange peel
⅔ cup sugar
2 eggs
1 cup self-rising flour
⅓ cup all-purpose flour
⅓ cup almond meal
½ cup sweetened dried cranberries
¼ cup orange juice
3 tablespoons milk

Modelling fondant

2 teaspoons gelatin
1⅓ tablespoons water
2 teaspoons simple syrup
1½ cups pure powdered sugar
½ cup pure powdered sugar, extra
yellow, orange and pink food coloring

Butter cream

6 tablespoons butter, softened
¼ teaspoon orange extract
1 cup powdered sugar
1½ tablespoons milk
yellow, orange and pink food coloring

1 Make modeling fondant; reserve a walnut-sized portion.
2 Dust surface with pure powdered sugar, roll remaining fondant to a thickness of approximately ⅛ inch. Cut out 18 flowers using 1¼-inch cutter or 36 flowers using ¾-inch cutter (see page 115).
3 Divide reserved fondant into three; knead one of the colorings into each portion. Roll tiny balls for flower centers; lightly brush flower centers with water to secure colored balls.
4 Preheat oven to 350°F. Line 6-hole oversize (Texas) or 12-hole standard muffin pan with paper baking cups.
5 Beat butter, orange peel, sugar and eggs in small bowl with electric mixer until light and fluffy.
6 Stir in sifted flours, almond meal, sweetened dried cranberries, orange juice and milk. Divide mixture among baking cups; smooth surface.
7 Bake large cakes about 35 minutes, small cakes about 25 minutes. Turn cakes onto wire rack to cool.
8 Make butter cream.
9 Spread cakes with butter cream; decorate with flowers.

Modelling fondant

Sprinkle gelatin over the water in cup; let stand cup in small pot of simmering water, stirring until gelatin is dissolved, add simple syrup. Place half the sifted powdered sugar in small bowl, stir in gelatin mixture. Gradually stir in remaining sifted powdered sugar, knead on surface dusted with extra sifted powdered sugar until smooth. Enclose in plastic wrap.

Butter cream

Beat butter and orange extract in small bowl with electric mixer until light and fluffy. Beat in sifted powdered sugar and milk, in two batches. Beat in a little of desired coloring.

neapolitan cakes

Marbled buttercake

1 stick butter, softened
½ teaspoon vanilla extract
⅔ cup sugar
2 eggs
1¼ cups self-rising flour
⅓ cup milk
pink food coloring
1½ tablespoons cocoa powder
2 teaspoons milk, extra

Butter cream

1 stick butter, softened
1½ cups powdered sugar
3 tablespoons milk
pink food coloring
1½ tablespoons cocoa powder
2 teaspoons milk, extra

1 Preheat oven to 350°F. Line 6-hole oversize (Texas) or 12-hole standard muffin pan with paper baking cups.

2 Beat butter, vanilla, sugar and eggs in small bowl with electric mixer until light and fluffy. Stir in sifted flour and milk, in two batches.

3 Divide mixture evenly among three bowls. Tint one mixture pink. Blend sifted cocoa with extra milk in cup; stir into another mixture. Leave third mixture plain.

4 Drop alternate spoonfuls of the three mixtures into baking cups. Pull a skewer backwards and forwards through mixtures for a marbled effect; smooth surface.

5 Bake large cakes about 30 minutes, small cakes about 20 minutes. Turn cakes onto wire rack to cool.

6 Make butter cream.

7 Spread cakes with the three colors of butter cream.

Butter cream

Beat butter in small bowl with electric mixer until as white as possible; beat in sifted powdered sugar and milk, in two batches. Divide mixture evenly among three bowls. Tint one mixture pink. Blend sifted cocoa with extra milk in cup; stir into another mixture. Leave third mixture plain.

kaleidocakes

Orange buttercake

6 tablespoons butter, softened
3 ounces cream cheese,
   softened
2 teaspoons finely grated
   orange peel
⅔ cup sugar
2 eggs
⅓ cup self-rising flour
½ cup all-purpose flour

Fondant icing

10½ ounces white prepared
   fondant, chopped coarsely
1 egg white
¼ teaspoon orange extract

Royal icing

1½ cups pure powdered sugar
1 egg white
½ teaspoon lemon juice
yellow, orange, green, pink and
   purple food coloring

1 Preheat oven to 350°F.
Line 6-hole oversize (Texas) or
12-hole standard muffin pan
with paper baking cups.
2 Beat butter, cheese, orange
peel, sugar and eggs in small
bowl with electric mixer until
light and fluffy.
3 Beat in flours on low speed
until just combined. Divide
mixture among baking cups;
smooth surface.
4 Bake large cakes about
30 minutes, small cakes about
20 minutes. Turn cakes onto
wire rack to cool.
5 Make fondant icing. Spread
over cakes; allow to set at
room temperature.
6 Make royal icing. Divide
evenly among five small bowls.
Using colorings, tint icing yellow,
orange, green, pink and purple;
cover each tightly with plastic
wrap. Pipe patterns (see page 122)
using picture as a guide.

Fondant icing

Place icing in a small bowl over a
small pot of simmering water; stir
until smooth. Stir in egg white
and orange extract. Let stand at
room temperature for 10 minutes
or until thickened slightly. Spread
fondant quickly over cakes; use
a metal spatula dipped in hot
water to smooth surface.

Royal icing

Sift powdered sugar through
very fine sieve. Lightly beat egg
white in small bowl with electric
mixer; add powdered sugar, a
tablespoon at a time. When
icing reaches firm peaks, use
wooden spoon to beat in
lemon juice; cover tightly with
plastic wrap.

banana caramel cakes

Sour cream banana cake
6 tablespoons butter, softened
½ cup firmly packed
   brown sugar
2 eggs
½ cup self-rising flour
½ cup all-purpose flour
½ teaspoon baking soda
½ teaspoon allspice
⅔ cup mashed overripe banana
⅓ cup sour cream
3 tablespoons milk

Filling and decorations
13-ounce jar caramel sauce
½ cup heavy cream, whipped
2 medium bananas (14 ounces),
   sliced thinly
3½ ounces dark chocolate

1 Preheat oven to 350°F.
Line 6-hole oversize (Texas) or
12-hole standard muffin pan
with paper baking cups.
2 Beat butter, sugar and eggs
in small bowl with electric mixer
until light and fluffy.
3 Stir in sifted dry ingredients,
banana, sour cream and milk.
Divide mixture among baking
cups; smooth surface.
4 Bake large cakes about
25 minutes, small cakes about
20 minutes. Turn cakes onto
wire rack to cool.
5 Remove baking cups
from cakes.
6 Fold 3 tablespoons of the
caramel into cream.
7 Cut cakes horizontally into
three slices. Re-assemble cakes
with remaining caramel and
banana. Top with caramel-
flavored cream.
8 Using a vegetable peeler,
grate chocolate (see page 116);
sprinkle over cakes.

lemon meringue cakes

Coconut lemon curd cake

1 stick butter, softened
2 teaspoons finely grated
  lemon peel
⅔ cup sugar
2 eggs
⅓ cup milk
¾ cup unsweetened
  shredded coconut
1¼ cups self-rising flour

Lemon curd

4 egg yolks
⅓ cup sugar
2 teaspoons finely grated
  lemon peel
¼ cup lemon juice
3 tablespoons butter

Coconut meringue

4 egg whites
1 cup sugar
1⅓ cups shredded coconut,
  chopped finely

1 Make lemon curd.
2 Preheat oven to 350°F.
Line 6-hole oversize (Texas) or
12-hole standard muffin pan
with paper baking cups.
3 Beat butter, lemon peel,
sugar and eggs in small bowl
with electric mixer until light
and fluffy.
4 Stir in milk and coconut, then
sifted flour. Divide mixture among
baking cups; smooth surface.
5 Bake large cakes about
25 minutes, small cakes about
20 minutes. Turn cakes onto
wire rack to cool. Increase oven
to 425°F.
6 Cut a ¾-inch deep hole in
the center of each cake, fill with
curd; discard cake tops.
7 Make coconut meringue;
spoon into a piping bag fitted
with a ½-inch plain tube.
8 Pipe meringue on top of each
cake (see page 122); place cakes
on baking sheet.
9 Bake in oven 5 minutes or
until meringue is browned lightly.

Lemon curd

Combine ingredients in a small
heatproof bowl over small pot
of simmering water, stirring
constantly, until mixture thickens
slightly and coats the back of a
spoon. Remove from heat. Cover
tightly; refrigerate curd until cold.

Coconut meringue

Beat egg whites in small bowl
with electric mixer until soft
peaks form; gradually add sugar,
beating until sugar dissolves.
Fold in coconut.

sweetheart

Pink petal dust can be purchased at specialty baking or cake-decorating shops.

Raspberry swirl cake

1 stick butter, softened
½ teaspoon vanilla extract
⅔ cup sugar
2 eggs
1¼ cups self-rising flour
⅓ cup milk
pink food coloring
3 tablespoons raspberry jam

Decorations

½ cup powdered sugar
12 ounces white prepared fondant
⅓ cup raspberry jam, warmed, strained
¼ teaspoon vodka
¼ teaspoon pink petal dust

1 Preheat oven to 350°F. Line 6-hole oversize (Texas) or 12-hole standard muffin pan with paper baking cups.

2 Beat butter, vanilla, sugar and eggs in small bowl with electric mixer until light and fluffy. Stir in sifted flour and milk, in two batches.

3 Divide mixture evenly between two bowls. Tint one mixture pink; leave other mixture plain. Drop alternate spoonfuls of the two mixtures into baking cups.

4 Divide jam among cakes, pull a skewer backwards and forwards through mixtures for a swirling effect; smooth surface.

5 Bake large cakes about 30 minutes, small cakes about 20 minutes. Turn cakes onto wire rack to cool.

6 On surface dusted with sifted powdered sugar, knead fondant until smooth. Tint fondant with pink coloring; knead into fondant only until marbled (see page 120). Roll out fondant to a thickness of ¼ inch. Cut out rounds large enough to cover tops of cakes.

7 Blend vodka with petal dust. Using a fine paint brush, paint mixture onto a heart-shaped rubber stamp; press lightly onto fondant rounds. Pinch edges of rounds with fingers.

8 Brush tops of cakes with jam; top with stamped rounds.

chocolate valentines

You can make your own almond meal by grinding blanched almonds in a nut mill or food processor until they reach the consistency of cornmeal.

Double chocolate raspberry cake

2 ounces dark chocolate, chopped coarsely
½ cup water
6 tablespoons butter, softened
1 cup firmly packed brown sugar
2 eggs
⅔ cup self-rising flour
3 tablespoons cocoa powder
⅓ cup almond meal
3½ ounces frozen raspberries

Decorations

3 tablespoons cocoa powder
2 pounds chocolate prepared fondant
⅓ cup raspberry jam, warmed, strained
½ cup powdered sugar
5 ounces red prepared fondant
5 ounces white prepared fondant
pink food coloring

1 Preheat oven to 325°F. Line 6-hole oversize (Texas) or 12-hole standard muffin pan with paper baking cups.
2 Combine chocolate and the water in small pot; stir over low heat until smooth.
3 Beat butter, sugar and eggs in small bowl with electric mixer until just combined.
4 Stir in sifted flour and cocoa, almond meal, then warm chocolate mixture; fold in raspberries. Divide among baking cups; smooth surface.
5 Bake large cakes about 55 minutes, small cakes about 45 minutes. Turn cakes onto wire rack to cool.
6 Remove baking cups from cakes. On a surface dusted with sifted cocoa, knead chocolate fondant until smooth. Roll out to a thickness of ¼-inch. Cut out rounds large enough to cover tops of cakes.
7 Brush cakes with jam; cover cakes with chocolate fondant.

8 On a surface dusted with sifted powdered sugar, knead white and red fondant separately until smooth. Use coloring to tint 3½ ounces of the white fondant pink (see page 120) and remaining white fondant a paler pink.
9 Roll each colored fondant to a thickness of ¼-inch. Using heart-shaped cutters of varying sizes (see page 115) to suit the size of cakes, cut out hearts from fondants using picture as a guide.
10 Decorate cakes with fondant hearts, each brushed with a little water to secure to each other.

coconut cherry hearts

Choc-chip cherry cake
1 stick butter, softened
½ teaspoon coconut extract
⅔ cup sugar
2 eggs
⅓ cup milk
½ cup unsweetened
   shredded coconut
⅓ cup red candied cherries,
   chopped coarsely
2 ounces dark chocolate,
   chopped coarsely
1 cup self-rising flour
¼ cup all-purpose flour

Milk chocolate ganache
¼ cup cream
3½ ounces milk chocolate,
   chopped coarsely

Decorations
5 ounces white chocolate
   chips, melted
pink food coloring

1 Preheat oven to 350°F.
Line 6-hole oversize (Texas) or
12-hole standard muffin pan
with paper baking cups.
2 Beat butter, coconut extract,
sugar and eggs in small bowl
with electric mixer until combined.
3 Stir in milk, coconut, cherries
and chocolate, then sifted flours.
Divide mixture among baking
cups; smooth surface.
4 Bake large cakes about
35 minutes, small cakes about
25 minutes. Turn cakes onto
wire rack to cool.
5 Make milk chocolate ganache.
6 Divide white chocolate evenly
among three small bowls; tint
two portions with two different
shades of pink (see page 117).
7 Make three paper piping bags
(see page 117); spoon a different
colored chocolate mixture into
each bag. Pipe different colored
heart shapes in varying sizes
(see page 117), onto parchment
paper-lined baking sheet. Set at
room temperature.
8 Spread cakes with ganache;
decorate with colored hearts.

Milk chocolate ganache
Bring cream to a boil in small
pot; pour over chocolate in small
bowl, stir until smooth. Cover;
let stand at room temperature
until ganache is spreadable.

the wedding story

It's important to measure the cake mixture carefully, so the cakes are all the same depth. Make the full amount of mixture; it will be fine standing at room temperature while you bake the 70 cakes in batches. We used standard sized foil baking cups. You will need 64 cakes for the story board. We used scrap booking decorations, available from craft stores.

White chocolate mud cake

1 pound butter,
    chopped coarsely
12 ounces white chocolate,
    chopped coarsely
4 cups sugar
2 cups milk
3 cups all-purpose flour
1 cup self-rising flour
2 teaspoons vanilla extract
4 eggs

Fluffy mock cream frosting

3 tablespoons milk
⅓ cup water
1 cup sugar
1 teaspoon gelatin
3 tablespoons water, extra
2 sticks butter, softened
1 teaspoon vanilla extract

Royal icing

1½ cups pure powdered sugar
1 egg white
½ teaspoon lemon juice

Decorations

24-inch square cake board
wedding-themed decorations
3 yards silver ribbon

1 Preheat oven to 325°F. Line two 12-hole standard muffin pans with baking cups.
2 Stir butter, chocolate, sugar and milk in large pot, over low heat, until smooth. Transfer to large bowl; cool 15 minutes.
3 Whisk in sifted flours then vanilla and eggs. Drop exactly 3 level tablespoons of mixture into each baking cup.
4 Bake cakes about 25 minutes. Turn onto wire rack to cool.
5 Meanwhile make fluffy mock cream frosting. Cover backs of decorations with parchment paper to prevent them from absorbing the frosting.
6 Spread 64 cakes with frosting, place on cake board. Secure ribbon around cakes.

7 Make royal icing; spoon icing into a piping bag fitted with a small plain tube. Pipe hearts onto about 10 of the cakes.
8 Top remaining cakes with wedding-themed decorations.

Fluffy mock cream frosting

Combine milk, the water and sugar in small pot, stir over low heat, without boiling, until sugar is dissolved. Sprinkle gelatin over extra water in cup, add to pot; stir syrup until gelatin is dissolved. Cool to room temperature. Beat butter and vanilla extract in small bowl with electric mixer, until as white as possible. While motor is running, gradually pour in cold syrup; beat until light and fluffy. Mixture will thicken on standing.

Royal icing

Sift powdered sugar through very fine sieve. Lightly beat egg white in small bowl with electric mixer; add powdered sugar, a tablespoon at a time. When icing reaches firm peaks, use a wooden spoon to beat in lemon juice; cover tightly with plastic wrap.

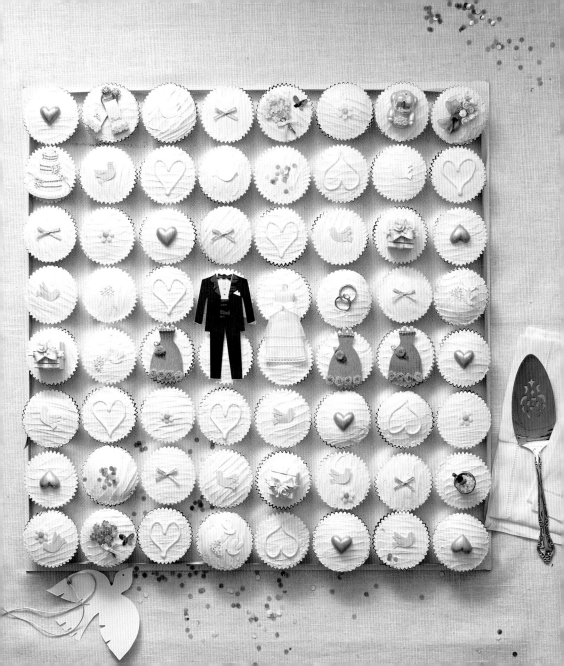

wedding
gift cakes

This cake is simply a stack of boxes each containing a cupcake for your wedding guests to take home. The choice of boxes, colors of ribbon and flowers is up to you. Choose the boxes first – size, color, and quantity. For the ribbon, measure each box, allowing enough ribbon to wrap around and overlap slightly. Our cake has been assembled directly onto a table, but you could also use a covered board. Choose flowers that complement the rest of the wedding flowers. We topped the boxes with a traditional cake for the bride and groom to cut. Alternatively, use a stunning arrangement of flowers. The first recipe explains what we did, using 54 cupcakes. This is only a guide – make the stack larger or smaller, or have more take-home boxes set aside. Most cupcake recipes in this book make 6 oversize (Texas) or 12 standard muffin-sized cakes, you will have to choose the size, type and flavor of cake you'd like, and then calculate how many batches of the recipe you'd need.

54 cupcakes
3½-inch square cake
4-inch square cake board
14 ounces white prepared fondant
¼ cup apricot jam,
    warmed, strained
14 ounces prepared almond paste
½ cup powdered sugar
22 yards ribbon
fifty-four 3-inch square gift boxes

1 Bake cupcakes for gift boxes and 3½-inch square cake of your choice.
2 Secure square cake to board with small piece of fondant made into a paste with water. Brush cake all over with jam.
3 Knead almond paste on surface dusted with sifted powdered sugar, cover cake (see page 110); let stand overnight.
4 Brush almond paste with jam, cover cake with fondant (see page 120); let stand overnight.
5 Secure ribbon to each box with glue or sticky tape.
6 Place one cupcake in each box; stack boxes. Position square cake on top. Decorate with flowers.

These recipes are for the cake on the top tier; use your favorite. All cakes are baked in a greased and lined deep 3½-inch square pan. A filigree textured plate was used to mark the fondant.

Rich fruit cake

5 tablespoons butter, softened
⅓ cup firmly packed
    brown sugar
1 egg
2 teaspoons orange marmalade
13 ounces (2⅓ cups) mixed
    dried fruit, chopped finely
⅓ cup all-purpose flour
¼ cup self-rising flour
½ teaspoon mixed spice
3 tablespoons sweet sherry
3 tablespoons sweet sherry,
    extra

1 Preheat oven to 275°F.
2 Follow method for Christmas snowflakes on page 111 for cake.
3 Bake cake about 2 hours.

White chocolate mud cake

5 tablespoons butter,
    chopped coarsely
1½ ounces white chocolate,
    chopped coarsely
½ cup sugar
¼ cup milk
⅓ cup all-purpose flour
3 tablespoons self-rising flour
½ teaspoon vanilla extract
1 egg, beaten lightly

1 Preheat oven to 325°F.
2 Follow method for Coconut kisses on page 35 for this cake.
3 Bake cake about 1 hour.

Dark chocolate mud cake

6 tablespoons butter,
    chopped coarsely
2 ounces dark chocolate,
    chopped coarsely
⅔ cup sugar
⅓ cup hot water
3 tablespoons coffee liqueur
1½ tablespoons instant
    coffee granules
½ cup all-purpose flour
1½ tablespoons self-rising flour
1½ tablespoons cocoa powder
1 egg, beaten lightly

1 Preheat oven to 325°F.
2 Follow method for Florentine cakes on page 43 for this cake.
3 Bake cake 1¾ hours.

This recipe makes three individual mini wedding cakes. Arrange the three together at different heights or levels (maybe even intertwined with flowers) for a lovely effect.

White chocolate and apricot mud cake

1 stick butter, chopped coarsely
3 ounces white chocolate, chopped coarsely
1 cup sugar
½ cup milk
¾ cup all-purpose flour
½ cup self-rising flour
½ cup finely chopped dried apricots
½ teaspoon vanilla extract
1 egg
⅓ cup apricot jam, warmed, strained
½ cup powdered sugar
2 pounds white prepared fondant

Modeling fondant

2 teaspoons gelatin
1⅓ tablespoons water
2 teaspoons simple syrup
1½ cups pure powdered sugar
½ cup pure powdered sugar, extra

Royal icing

1½ cups pure powdered sugar
1 egg white
½ teaspoon lemon juice

1 Make modeling fondant. On a surface dusted with extra powdered sugar, roll fondant to approximately ⅛-inch thickness. Cut out flowers using 1½-inch and ½-inch cutters (see page 115). Shape flowers using a ball tool (see pages 120 and 115); dry on dish towel.
2 Preheat oven to 325°F. Line 6-hole oversize (Texas) muffin pan with paper baking cups.
3 Combine butter, chocolate, sugar and milk in small pot; stir over low heat, until smooth. Transfer mixture to medium bowl; cool 15 minutes.
4 Whisk in sifted flours, apricots, then vanilla and egg; divide mixture among baking cups.
5 Bake cakes about 45 minutes. Turn cakes onto wire rack to cool.
6 Meanwhile make royal icing. Spoon icing into piping bag fitted with small plain tube, keep icing covered with a damp cloth.
7 Remove baking cups from cakes. Trim cake edges to make neat cylindrical shapes when stacked. Join two trimmed cakes with apricot jam; brush cakes all over with remaining jam.
8 On surface dusted with sifted powdered sugar, knead fondant until smooth. Divide fondant into three equal portions. Roll out each portion to a thickness of ¼ inch.

Cover the three cake stacks individually with fondant. Trim bases and smooth fondant (see page 120).
9 Pipe a little royal icing onto the back of each flower; secure to cake. Pipe some dots in the center of each flower and around the base of each cake.

Modeling fondant

Sprinkle gelatin over the water in cup; place cup in small pot of simmering water, stirring until gelatin is dissolved; add simple syrup. Place half the sifted powdered sugar in medium bowl, stir in gelatin mixture. Gradually stir in remaining sifted powdered sugar. Knead on surface dusted with extra sifted powdered sugar until smooth. Wrap tightly in plastic wrap to prevent drying out.

Royal icing

Sift powdered sugar through very fine sieve. Lightly beat egg white in small bowl with electric mixer; add powdered sugar, a tablespoon at a time. When icing reaches firm peaks, use a wooden spoon to beat in lemon juice; cover tightly with plastic wrap.

white wedding

lily wedding cakes

Rich fruit cake

6 tablespoons butter, softened
½ cup firmly packed
  brown sugar
2 eggs
1½ tablespoons orange
  marmalade
1 pound (2¾ cups) mixed dried
  fruit, chopped finely
⅔ cup all-purpose flour
3 tablespoons self-rising flour
1 teaspoon allspice
3 tablespoons sweet sherry
3 tablespoons sweet sherry, extra

Modeling fondant

2 teaspoons gelatin
1⅓ tablespoons water
2 teaspoons simple syrup
1½ cups pure powdered sugar
½ cup pure powdered sugar, extra

Royal icing

1½ cups pure powdered sugar
1 egg white
½ teaspoon lemon juice

Decorations

⅓ cup apricot jam,
  warmed, strained
½ cup powdered sugar
2 pounds white prepared fondant
covered 22 gauge wire
florist tape
30 stamens

1 Make modeling fondant. On surface dusted with extra sifted powdered sugar, roll a little of the fondant to approximately ⅛-inch thickness. Cut out petals using lily petal cutter (see pages 115 and 121) allowing 6 petals for each cake. Vary size of petals to suit size of cakes. Using frilling tool (see pages 115 and 121), gently shape petals; attach damp 4-inch length wire to each petal (see pages 115 and 121); allow to dry (see page 121).
2 Preheat oven to 275°F. Line 6-hole oversize (Texas) or 12-hole standard muffin pan with paper baking cups.
3 Beat butter, sugar and eggs in small bowl with electric mixer until just combined.
4 Transfer mixture to medium bowl; add marmalade and fruit, mix well.
5 Sift flours and spice over mixture; add sherry, mix well. Divide mixture among baking cups; smooth surface.
6 Bake large cakes about 1 hour, small cakes about 50 minutes. Remove cakes from oven; brush tops with extra sherry. Cover pan tightly with foil; cool cakes in pan.
7 Meanwhile, assemble lilies using royal icing, stamens and pistles (see page 121).
8 Remove baking cups from cakes. Brush cakes with jam. On surface dusted with sifted powdered sugar, knead

prepared fondant until smooth. Divide fondant into six or 12 equal portions. Roll out each portion to a thickness of ¼ inch. Cover cakes with fondant; trim base and smooth fondant (see page 120).
9 Make royal icing. Spoon royal icing into piping bag fitted with small plain tube. Pipe a continuous line in a cornelli pattern over cakes (see page 122). Secure lilies to cakes.

Modeling fondant

Sprinkle gelatin over the water in cup; place cup in small pot of simmering water, stirring until gelatin is dissolved, add simple syrup. Sift half the powdered sugar in medium bowl, stir in gelatin mixture. Gradually stir in remaining sifted powdered sugar, knead on surface dusted with extra sifted powdered sugar until smooth. Wrap tightly in plastic wrap to prevent drying out.

Royal icing

Sift powdered sugar through very fine sieve. Lightly beat egg white in small bowl; add powdered sugar, a tablespoon at a time, beating well after each addition. When icing reaches firm peaks, add lemon juice; beat well. Cover tightly with plastic wrap.

If your oven won't hold three sets of muffin pans, it's fine to leave the mixture standing at room temperature while the first batch bakes. We used three cake stands stacked on top of each other to display the cakes. They measured 6½ inches, 10 inches and 13 inches in diameter. We used a plastic filigree textured plate to mark the icing, available from craft stores. Mix and match the colors of the plates, cakes and flowers to suit the occasion. Silver luster can be found at specialty baking and cake-decorating shops.

Rich fruit cake

2 sticks butter, softened
1¼ cups firmly packed
    brown sugar
4 eggs
3 tablespoons orange
    marmalade
3½ pounds mixed dried fruit,
    chopped finely
1½ cups all-purpose flour
½ cup self-rising flour
2 teaspoons allspice
½ cup sweet sherry
¼ cup blanched whole almonds
3 tablespoons sweet sherry, extra

Decorations

½ cup powdered sugar
1¾ pounds white
    prepared fondant
filigree textured plate
½ cup orange marmalade,
    warmed, strained
silver luster

1 Preheat oven to 275°F. Line three 12-hole standard muffin pans with silver foil and paper baking cups.
2 Beat butter, sugar and eggs in small bowl with electric mixer until just combined.
3 Transfer mixture to large bowl, add marmalade and fruit; mix well.
4 Sift flours and spice over mixture, add sherry; mix well.
5 Place 3 level tablespoons of mixture into baking cups; smooth surface.
6 Bake cakes about 50 minutes. Remove cakes from oven; brush tops with extra sherry. Cover pan tightly with foil; cool cakes in pan.
7 On surface dusted with sifted powdered sugar, knead fondant until smooth. Roll out to a thickness of ¼ inch. Using a 3-inch round fluted cutter cut out 36 rounds.
8 Using a filigree textured plate (see page 115), gently press an imprint onto each fondant round (see page 125).
9 Brush cakes with marmalade; top with fondant rounds. Carefully brush silver luster over pattern on fondant.

lace wedding cakes

deluxe chocolate wedding

You need to buy triple the quantity of the ingredients for the cake recipe below. You will need to make three separate batches, do not double or triple this recipe. It's important to measure the cake mixture carefully so the cakes are all the same depth. The mixture will be fine standing at room temperature while you bake the cakes in batches. Each batch will make 40 cakes. You will need 120 standard muffin paper baking cups.

Mocha mud cake

1 pound butter, chopped coarsely
10½ ounces dark chocolate, chopped coarsely
4 cups sugar
2 cups water
⅔ cup coffee liqueur
3 tablespoons instant coffee granules
3 cups all-purpose flour
½ cup self-rising flour
½ cup cocoa powder
4 eggs

Dark chocolate ganache

3 cups heavy cream
1¾ pounds dark chocolate, chopped coarsely

Decorations

6-inch, 8-inch, 12-inch, 14-inch and 18-inch round boards
5½ yards ½-inch cotton lace ribbon
4 empty cans, 3½ inches tall and 2 inches in diameter
wrapping paper, for cans
7 ounces milk chocolate
½ cup finely chopped candied ginger
½ cup dried rose petals
¼ cup roasted coffee beans
2 miniature brandy snaps or ginger snaps

1 Preheat oven to 325°F. Line two 12-hole standard muffin pans with paper baking cups.
2 Combine butter, chocolate, sugar, the water, liqueur and coffee in large pot; stir over low heat until smooth. Transfer mixture to large bowl; cool 15 minutes.
3 Whisk in sifted flours and cocoa, then eggs. Pour exactly ¼ cup of mixture into each case.
4 Bake cakes about 40 minutes. Turn cakes onto wire racks to cool.
5 Make dark chocolate ganache.
6 Attach ribbon to edge of round boards, using double sided tape. Cover cans with wrapping paper. Glue cans to center of the four largest boards. Stack boards from the bottom tier up, as shown in picture.
7 Spread all cakes with ganache. Decorate cakes as shown with chocolate curls using vegetable peeler (see page 116), candied ginger, coffee beans, rose petals and brandy snaps.
8 Place cakes on boards.

Dark chocolate ganache
Bring cream to a boil in medium pot, pour over chocolate in large bowl; stir until smooth. Cover bowl; refrigerate, about 30 minutes or until ganache is of a spreadable consistency.

You can make your own almond meal by grinding blanched almonds in a nut mill or food processor until they reach the consistency of cornmeal.

1 stick plus 2 tablespoons butter, softened
½ teaspoon almond extract
⅔ cup sugar
2 eggs
⅓ cup self-rising flour
½ cup all-purpose flour
½ cup almond meal

5 tablespoons butter
¾ cup water
¾ cup all-purpose flour
3 eggs, beaten lightly

1¼ cups milk
1 vanilla bean, split
4 egg yolks
½ cup sugar
¼ cup cornstarch

1 cup sugar
½ cup water

1 Make choux pastry; make vanilla custard.

2 Preheat oven to 350°F. Line 6-hole oversize (Texas) muffin or 12-hole standard pan with paper baking cups.

3 Beat butter, extract, sugar and eggs in small bowl with electric mixer until light and fluffy.

4 Stir in sifted flours and almond meal, in two batches. Divide mixture among baking cups; smooth surface.

5 Bake large cakes about 30 minutes, small cakes about 20 minutes. Turn cakes onto wire rack to cool.

6 Cut a ¾-inch deep hole in the center of each cake, fill with custard; replace lid.

7 Spread tops of cakes with a little more custard. Top with a layer of puffs. Stack remaining puffs on cakes dipping each in a little custard.

8 Make toffee; drizzle over puffs.

Preheat oven to 425°F. Grease baking sheets, line with parchment paper. Combine butter with the water in medium pot; bring to a boil. Add flour; beat with wooden spoon over medium heat until mixture forms a smooth ball. Transfer mixture to small bowl; beat in egg with electric mixer in about six batches until mixture becomes glossy. Spoon mixture into piping bag fitted with ½-inch plain tube. Pipe about 300 tiny dollops of pastry (about ¼ level teaspoon) ¾-inch apart, onto trays (see page 122); bake 7 minutes. Reduce oven to 350°F; bake another 5 minutes or until puffs are crisp. Repeat with remaining mixture.

Bring milk and vanilla bean to a boil in small pot; discard vanilla bean. Meanwhile, beat egg yolks, sugar and cornstarch in small bowl with electric mixer until thick. With motor running, gradually beat in warm milk. Return custard to same pot; stir over medium heat until mixture boils and thickens. Cover surface of custard with plastic wrap; cool.

Combine sugar with the water in small heavy-based pot. Stir over medium heat, without boiling, until sugar dissolves; bring to a boil. Reduce heat; simmer, uncovered, without stirring, until mixture is golden brown. Remove from heat; let stand until bubbles subside before using.

toffee tumbles

apple custard tea cakes

Apple custard tea cakes

6 tablespoons butter
½ teaspoon vanilla extract
½ cup sugar
2 eggs
¾ cup self-rising flour
¼ cup instant vanilla
　　pudding mix
3 tablespoons milk
1 large (7 ounces) unpeeled
　　apple, cored, sliced finely
2 tablespoons butter,
　　extra, melted
1½ tablespoons sugar, extra
½ teaspoon ground cinnamon

Custard

1½ tablespoons instant vanilla
　　pudding mix
1½ tablespoons sugar
½ cup milk
¼ teaspoon vanilla extract

1 Make custard.
2 Preheat oven to 350°F.
Line 6-hole oversize (Texas) or
12-hole standard muffin pan
with paper baking cups.
3 Beat butter, vanilla, sugar,
eggs, flour, pudding mix and
milk in small bowl with electric
mixer on low speed until
ingredients are just combined.
Increase speed to medium,
beat until mixture is changed
to a paler color.
4 Divide half the mixture among
baking cups. Top with custard,
then remaining cake mixture;
spread mixture to cover custard.
Top with apple slices, pressing
slightly into cake.
5 Bake large cakes about
40 minutes, small cakes about
30 minutes.
6 Brush hot cakes with extra
butter, then sprinkle with
combined extra sugar and
cinnamon. Turn cakes onto wire
rack. Serve warm or cold.

Custard

Blend pudding mix and sugar
with milk and vanilla in small
pot; stir over medium heat until
mixture boils and thickens.
Remove from heat; cover surface
with plastic wrap; cool.

flower cakes

6½ tablespoons butter,
  softened
½ cup firmly packed
  brown sugar
2 eggs
½ cup self-rising flour
½ cup all-purpose flour
½ teaspoon baking soda
½ teaspoon allspice
⅔ cup mashed overripe banana
⅓ cup sour cream
3 tablespoons milk

Modeling fondant

2 teaspoons gelatin
1½ tablespoons water
2 teaspoons simple syrup
1½ cups powdered sugar
½ cup powdered sugar, extra

Cream cheese frosting

2 tablespoons butter, softened
3 ounces cream cheese,
  softened
1½ cups powdered sugar
blue food coloring

Decorations

½ cup icing sugar
14 ounces white prepared
  fondant
pink and yellow food coloring
pink petal dust

1 Make modeling fondant. On a surface dusted with extra sifted powdered sugar, roll modeling fondant to approximately ⅛-inch thick. Cut out butterfly wings using butterfly cutter and shape butterfly bodies (see page 120); allow to dry.

2 Preheat oven to 350°F. Line 6-hole oversize or 12-hole standard muffin pan with paper baking cups.

3 Beat butter, sugar and eggs in small bowl with electric mixer until light and fluffy.

4 Stir in sifted dry ingredients, then banana, sour cream and milk. Divide mixture among baking cups; smooth surface.

5 Bake large cakes about 35 minutes, small cakes about 25 minutes. Turn cakes onto wire rack to cool.

6 Make cream cheese frosting. Assemble butterflies (see pages 120 and 121).

7 On surface dusted with sifted powdered sugar, knead prepared fondant until smooth. Using coloring, tint three-quarters of the fondant pink and one-quarter yellow. Roll out pink fondant to a thickness of ¼ inch; cut out petal shapes to suit the size of the cakes. Shape yellow fondant into balls; gently flatten until large enough to form center of flowers.

8 Spread cakes with frosting. Decorate with petals and centers. Position a butterfly on each cake; dust wings with pink petal dust (see page 115).

Modelling fondant

Sprinkle gelatin over the water in cup; stand cup in small saucepan of simmering water, stirring until gelatin is dissolved; add simple syrup. Sift half the powdered sugar into medium bowl; stir in gelatin mixture. Gradually stir in remaining sifted powdered sugar, knead on surface dusted with extra sifted powdered sugar until smooth. Wrap tightly in plastic wrap to prevent drying out.

Cream cheese frosting

Beat butter and cheese in small bowl with electric mixer until light and fluffy; gradually beat in sifted powdered sugar. Tint with coloring.

You can make your own hazelnut meal by grinding skinned hazelnuts in a nut mill or food processor until they reach the consistency of cornmeal.

3½ ounces dark chocolate
   chips, melted
⅓ cup chocolate hazelnut spread
¼ cup hazelnut meal
1½ tablespoons finely crushed
   ice cream cones
12 hazelnuts, toasted
1½ tablespoons hazelnut
   meal, extra

1 Using small, clean paint brush, paint chocolate thickly inside 12 miniature foil baking cups. Place baking cups on tray; refrigerate about 5 minutes or until chocolate sets. Peel away baking cups (see pages 116 and 117).

2 Combine spread and hazelnut meal in small bowl; spoon mixture into piping bag fitted with ½-inch fluted tube.

3 Divide pieces of wafer and hazelnuts among baking cups. Pipe chocolate mixture into baking cups. Sprinkle with extra hazelnut meal.

chocolate hazelnut cups

We used green, orange and yellow paper baking cups to match the decorations of these lovely cakes. You can make your own almond meal by grinding blanched almonds in a nut mill or food processor until they reach the consistency of cornmeal.

Poppy seed citrus cake

¼ cup poppy seeds
3 tablespoons milk
1 stick butter, softened
1 teaspoon finely grated lemon peel
1 teaspoon finely grated lime peel
⅔ cup sugar
2 eggs
1 cup self-rising flour
⅓ cup all-purpose flour
⅓ cup almond meal
¼ cup orange juice

Decorations

½ cup powdered sugar
1 pound white prepared fondant
green, orange and yellow food coloring
⅓ cup orange marmalade, warmed, strained
3 tablespoons green sprinkles
3 tablespoons orange sprinkles
3 tablespoons yellow sprinkles

1 Preheat oven to 350°F. Line 6-hole oversize (Texas) or 12-hole standard muffin pan with paper baking cups.
2 Combine seeds and milk in small bowl; let stand 20 minutes.
3 Beat butter, peels, sugar and eggs in small bowl with electric mixer until light and fluffy.
4 Stir in sifted flours, almond meal, orange juice and poppy seed mixture. Divide mixture among baking cups; smooth the surface.
5 Bake large cakes about 30 minutes, small cakes about 20 minutes. Turn cakes onto wire rack to cool.
6 On surface dusted with sifted powdered sugar, knead fondant until smooth. Reserve 3½ ounces of fondant; enclose in plastic wrap. Divide remaining fondant into three equal portions; tint green, orange and yellow by kneading in coloring (see page 120). Wrap separately in plastic wrap.

7 Roll each of the colored portions to a thickness of ¼ inch. Cut out rounds large enough to cover tops of cakes. Brush tops of cakes with marmalade, position rounds on cakes.
8 Roll reserved fondant into very thin lengths, cut off small pieces to represent seeds. Position lengths on top of cakes, using a little water, to represent segments.
9 Fill segments with matching colored sprinkles; position fondant seeds.

sweet violet cakes

Lemon cream cheese cake

6 tablespoons butter, softened
3 ounces cream cheese,
   softened
2 teaspoons finely grated
   lemon peel
⅔ cup sugar
2 eggs
⅓ cup self-rising flour
½ cup all-purpose flour

Lemon cream cheese frosting

2 tablespoons butter, softened
3 ounces cream cheese,
   softened
1 teaspoon finely grated
   lemon peel
1½ cups powdered sugar

Decorations

tea-lights
fresh violets

1 Preheat oven to 350°F.
Line 6-hole oversize (Texas) or
12-hole standard muffin pan
with paper baking cups.
2 Beat butter, cheese, lemon
peel, sugar and eggs in small
bowl with electric mixer until
light and fluffy.
3 Add sifted flours; beat on
low speed until just combined.
Divide mixture among baking
cups; smooth surface.
4 Bake large cakes about
35 minutes, small cakes about
25 minutes. Turn cakes onto
wire rack to cool.
5 Make lemon cream cheese
frosting. Spread cakes with
frosting; decorate with tea-lights
and violets.

Lemon cream cheese frosting

Beat butter, cream cheese and
lemon peel in small bowl with
electric mixer until light and
fluffy; gradually beat in sifted
powdered sugar.

Cherry chocolate mud cake

15-ounce can pitted cherries
   in syrup
1 stick plus 3 tablespoons,
   chopped coarsely
3½ ounces dark chocolate,
   chopped coarsely
1⅓ cups sugar
¼ cup cherry brandy
1 cup all-purpose flour
3 tablespoons self-rising flour
3 tablespoons cocoa powder
1 egg

Decorations

⅔ cup heavy cream, whipped
2 teaspoons cherry brandy
3½ ounces dark chocolate

black forest cakes

1 Preheat oven to 325°F.
Line 6-hole oversize (Texas) or
12-hole standard muffin pan
with paper baking cups.
2 Drain cherries; reserve syrup.
Process ½ cup cherries with
½ cup of the syrup until smooth.
Halve remaining cherries; reserve
for decorating cakes. Discard
remaining syrup.
3 Combine butter, chocolate,
sugar, brandy and cherry puree
in small pot; stir over low heat
until chocolate is melted.
Transfer mixture to medium
bowl; cool 15 minutes.
4 Whisk in sifted flours and
cocoa, then egg. Divide mixture
among baking cups; smooth
the surface.
5 Bake large cakes about
55 minutes, small cakes about
45 minutes. Turn cakes onto
wire rack to cool.
6 Top cakes with remaining
cherry halves and combined
cream and cherry brandy. Using
a vegetable peeler, make small
chocolate curls (see page 116);
sprinkle over cakes.

passion fruit curd cakes

Passion fruit buttercake

6 tablespoons butter, softened
½ cup sugar
2 eggs
1 cup self-rising flour
¼ cup passion fruit pulp

Passion fruit curd

2 eggs, beaten lightly
⅓ cup sugar
1½ tablespoons lemon juice
¼ cup passion fruit pulp
5 tablespoons butter,
  chopped coarsely

Decorations

3-ounce packet tropical
  fruit Jell-O
1 cup boiling water
1 cup unsweetened
  shredded coconut
½ cup heavy cream, whipped

1 Make passion fruit curd.

2 Preheat oven to 350°F.
Line 6-hole oversize (Texas) or
12-hole standard muffin pan
with paper baking cups.

3 Beat butter, sugar, eggs
and flour in small bowl with
electric mixer on low speed until
ingredients are just combined.
Increase speed to medium, beat
until mixture is changed to a paler
color. Stir in passion fruit pulp.

4 Divide mixture among baking
cups; smooth surface.

5 Bake large cakes about
25 minutes, small cakes about
20 minutes. Turn cakes onto
wire rack to cool.

6 Dissolve Jell-O in the water.
Refrigerate about 30 minutes or
until set to the consistency of
unbeaten egg white.

7 Remove baking cups from
cakes. Roll cakes in Jell-O; leave
cakes to let stand in Jell-O for
15 minutes turning occasionally.
Roll cakes in coconut; place on
wire rack over tray. Refrigerate
30 minutes.

8 Cut cakes in half; fill with curd
and cream.

Passion fruit curd

Combine ingredients in a small
heatproof bowl, place over a
small pot of simmering water;
stir constantly until mixture
thickens slightly and coats the
back of a spoon. Remove from
heat. Cover tightly; refrigerate
curd until cold.

You can make your own almond meal by grinding blanched almonds in a nut mill or food processor until they reach the consistency of cornmeal.

Orange almond cake

6 slices candied orange
5 tablespoons butter, softened
1 teaspoon finely grated
   orange peel
⅓ cup sugar
1 egg
3 tablespoons self-rising flour
¼ cup all-purpose flour
¼ cup almond meal

Decorations

6-inch styrofoam craft ball
24 wooden toothpicks
2 sheets tissue paper
ribbon
fresh flowers
florist tape

1 Cut each orange slice into 20 tiny wedges.
2 Preheat oven to 350°F. Line two 12-hole mini muffin pans with paper baking cups.
3 Beat butter, orange peel, sugar and egg in small bowl with electric mixer until light and fluffy.
4 Stir in sifted flours and almond meal. Divide mixture among baking cups; smooth surface. Top each cake with five orange wedges.
5 Bake cakes about 15 minutes. Turn cakes onto wire rack to cool.
6 Using a serrated knife cut about quarter of the ball away, so the ball will sit flat. Using toothpicks, secure cakes to ball. Place bouquet on a small stand; wrap with paper and ribbon. Bind ends of fresh flowers with florist tape; position flowers between cakes.

orange bouquet

no-bake chocolate cakes

five 2-ounce mars bars
4 tablespoons butter
3½ cups crispy rice cereal
7 ounces milk chocolate, melted

1 Line a 12-hole standard muffin pan with paper baking cups.
2 Chop four mars bars coarsely; cut remaining bar into slices.
3 Place chopped bars in medium pot with butter; stir over low heat until smooth. Stir in rice bubbles.
4 Press mixture into baking cups, spread with chocolate; top with sliced mars bar. Refrigerate 30 minutes or until set.

pineapple hibiscus cakes

Pineapple carrot cake

½ cup vegetable oil
3 eggs, beaten lightly
1½ cups self-rising flour
¾ cup sugar
½ teaspoon ground cinnamon
2 cups firmly packed coarsely grated carrot
¾ cup drained crushed pineapple

Pineapple flowers

1½ tablespoons sugar
1½ tablespoons water
12 wafer thin slices fresh pineapple

Lemon cream cheese frosting

2 tablespoons butter, softened
3 ounces cream cheese, softened
1 teaspoon finely grated lemon peel
1½ cups powdered sugar

1 Make pineapple flowers.
2 Preheat oven to 350°F. Line a 6-hole oversize (Texas) or 12-hole standard muffin pan with paper baking cups.
3 Combine oil, eggs, flour, sugar and cinnamon in medium bowl; stir until combined. Stir in carrot and pineapple.
4 Divide mixture among baking cups.
5 Bake large cakes about 40 minutes, small cakes about 30 minutes. Turn cakes onto wire rack to cool.
6 Make lemon cream cheese frosting; spread on top of cakes. Decorate with pineapple flowers.

Pineapple flowers

Preheat oven to 250°F. Stir sugar and the water together in a small pot over low heat until sugar has dissolved; boil 1 minute. Brush both sides of pineapple slices with sugar syrup. Place slices in a single layer on wire racks over baking sheets (see page 125). Dry pineapple in oven for about 1 hour. Immediately remove slices from rack; carefully shape into flowers. Dry over an egg carton (see page 125).

Lemon cream cheese frosting

Beat butter, cream cheese and lemon peel in small bowl with electric mixer until light and fluffy; gradually beat in sifted powdered sugar.

chocolate ginger gum nuts

Ginger wine is a traditional Scottish beverage; if you have trouble finding it, you can substitute with dry vermouth.

Chocolate ginger mud cake
1 stick plus 3 tablespoons butter, chopped coarsely
3½ ounces dark chocolate, chopped coarsely
1⅓ cups sugar
⅔ cup green ginger wine
¼ cup water
1 cup all-purpose flour
3 tablespoons self-rising flour
3 tablespoons cocoa powder
1 egg
⅓ cup finely chopped candied ginger

Chocolate decorations
3½ ounces dark chocolate chips, melted
3½ ounces milk chocolate chips, melted
fresh rose leaves, washed

Dark chocolate ganache
½ cup heavy cream
7 ounces dark chocolate, chopped coarsely

1 Make chocolate decorations – gum nuts, branches and leaves.
2 Preheat oven to 325°F. Line 6-hole oversize (Texas) or 12-hole standard muffin pan with paper baking cups.
3 Combine butter, chocolate, sugar, wine and the water in small pot; stir over low heat until smooth. Transfer to medium bowl; cool 15 minutes.
4 Whisk in sifted flours and cocoa, then egg. Stir in chopped ginger. Divide mixture among baking cups.
5 Bake large cakes about 1 hour, small cakes about 50 minutes. Turn cakes onto wire rack to cool.
6 Make dark chocolate ganache.
7 Pour ganache over cakes; set at room temperature.
8 Decorate cakes with chocolate gum nuts, branches and leaves.

Chocolate decorations
For gum nuts, spread dark chocolate onto a cold surface; when set, pull a melon baller over chocolate to make gum nuts (see page 116). For branches, spoon half the milk chocolate into paper piping bag (see page 117); pipe branches onto a parchment paper-lined tray (see page 117); leave to set. Gently lift branches off paper. For leaves, using a small, clean paint brush, paint remaining milk chocolate thickly on one side of each leaf (see page 116), place on parchment paper-lined tray; leave to set. Carefully peel away and discard leaves (see page 117).

Dark chocolate ganache
Bring cream to a boil in small pot; pour over chocolate in small bowl, stir until smooth. Let stand at room temperature until ganache becomes a thick pouring consistency.

easter egg baskets

Light fruit cake

1 stick butter, softened
½ teaspoon almond extract
⅔ cup sugar
2 eggs
⅔ cup red and green candied
 cherries, quartered
⅓ cup sultanas
½ cup slivered almonds
⅔ cup all-purpose flour
⅓ cup self-rising flour
¼ cup milk

Royal icing

3 cups powered sugar
2 egg whites
1 teaspoon lemon juice
brown food coloring

Decorations

10½ ounces candied almonds
 or mini chocolate eggs

1 Preheat oven to 325°F.
Line 6-hole oversize (Texas) or
12-hole standard muffin pan
with paper baking cups.
2 Beat butter, extract, sugar and
eggs in small bowl with electric
mixer until light and fluffy.
3 Add fruit and nuts; mix well.
Stir in sifted flours and milk.
Divide mixture among cases;
smooth surface.
4 Bake large cakes about
45 minutes, small cakes about
40 minutes. Turn cakes onto
wire rack to cool.
5 Make royal icing.
6 Remove cases from cakes.
Pipe basket weave around cakes
(see page 123); leave to dry for
3 hours or overnight.
7 Fill baskets with candied
almonds or chocolate eggs.

Royal icing

Sift powered sugar through
very fine sieve. Lightly beat egg
whites in small bowl with electric
mixer; beat in powered sugar,
a tablespoon at a time. When
icing reaches firm peaks, use
wooden spoon to beat in juice
and coloring; cover tightly with
plastic wrap.

spicy Christmas cakes

Make these festive cupcakes for Christmas; serve warm with brandy butter, whipped cream or custard.

Buttermilk spice cake
½ cup firmly packed
   brown sugar
½ cup all-purpose flour
½ cup self-rising flour
¼ teaspoon baking soda
1 teaspoon ground ginger
½ teaspoon ground cinnamon
¼ teaspoon ground nutmeg
6 tablespoons butter, softened
1 egg
¼ cup buttermilk
3 tablespoons honey

Christmas decorations
½ cup powdered sugar
3½ ounces white prepared
   fondant
2-inch lengths of covered
   24 gauge wire

Filling
½ cup mincemeat
1½ tablespoons powdered sugar

1 Make Christmas decorations.
2 Preheat oven to 350°F. Line 6-hole oversize (Texas) or 12-hole standard muffin pan with paper baking cups.
3 Sift dry ingredients into small bowl, add remaining ingredients; beat with electric mixer on low speed until ingredients are combined. Increase speed to medium, beat until mixture is smooth and changed to a paler color. Divide mixture among baking cups; smooth surface.
4 Bake large cakes about 35 minutes, small cakes about 25 minutes. Turn cakes onto wire rack to cool for 5 minutes.
5 Cut a ¾-inch deep hole in the center of each warm cake; discard cake rounds. Fill centers with mincemeat mixture. Top with wired fondant shapes; dust with a little sifted powdered sugar.

Christmas decorations
On surface dusted with sifted powdered sugar, knead fondant until smooth. Roll out to ½-inch thickness. Cut out fondant shapes using Christmas cutters (see page 115). Insert a length of damp wire into each shape. Dry overnight on parchment paper-lined tray.

Filling
Warm mincemeat in small pot over low heat; stir in powdered sugar. Or, heat mincemeat in a microwave oven for about 30 seconds on high (100%); stir in powdered sugar.

Christmas tree cakes

Put a tropical twist on Christmas with these pretty little cakes.

Tropical fruit cake

1 stick butter, softened
1 teaspoon coconut extract
⅔ cup sugar
2 eggs
1 cup finely chopped dried
   tropical fruit salad
½ cup macadamia nuts,
   chopped coarsely
⅔ cup all-purpose flour
⅓ cup self-rising flour
⅓ cup unsweetened
   shredded coconut
¼ cup milk

Coconut frosting

2 egg whites
1 teaspoon coconut extract
1½ cups powdered sugar
1 cup unsweetened
   shredded coconut

Decorations

10 star fruit, approximately
green edible glitter

1 Preheat oven to 325°F. Line 6-hole oversize (Texas) or 12-hole standard muffin pan with paper baking cups.
2 Beat butter, vanilla, sugar and eggs in small bowl with electric mixer until light and fluffy.
3 Stir in dried fruit and nuts, then sifted flours, coconut and milk. Divide mixture among baking cups; smooth surface.
4 Bake large cakes about 45 minutes, small cakes about 35 minutes. Turn cakes onto wire racks to cool.
5 Make coconut frosting; top cakes with frosting.
6 Cut star fruit into ¼-inch slices. Arrange slices to make Christmas tree shapes of varying heights and sizes depending on size of cakes used. Use toothpicks or trimmed bamboo skewers to hold star fruit in position. Sprinkle with glitter.

Coconut frosting

Beat egg whites and coconut extract in small bowl with electric mixer until foamy. Beat in sifted powdered sugar in about four batches; stir in coconut.

Christmas snowflakes

Silver luster and cachous can be found at specialty baking and cake-decorating stores.

Rich fruit cake

6 tablespoons butter, softened
½ cup firmly packed brown sugar
2 eggs
1½ tablespoons orange marmalade
1 pound mixed dried fruit, chopped finely
⅔ cup all-purpose flour
3 tablespoons self-rising flour
1 teaspoon allspice
3 tablespoons sweet sherry
3 tablespoons sweet sherry, extra

Decorations

½ cup powdered sugar
10½ ounces white prepared fondant
½ teaspoon silver luster
½ teaspoon vodka
silver cachous
⅓ cup apricot jam, warmed, strained

1 Preheat oven to 275°F. Line 6-hole oversize (Texas) or 12-hole standard muffin pan with paper baking cups.

2 Beat butter, sugar and eggs in small bowl with electric mixer until just combined.

3 Stir in marmalade and fruit; mix well.

4 Sift flours and spice over mixture; add sherry, mix well. Divide mixture among baking cups; smooth surface.

5 Bake large cakes about 1 hour, small cakes about 50 minutes. Remove cakes from oven; brush tops with extra sherry. Cover pan tightly with foil; cool cakes in pan.

6 On surface dusted with sifted powdered sugar, knead fondant until smooth; roll out to a thickness of ¼ inch. Using a fluted cutter, cut out rounds large enough to almost cover tops of cakes.

7 Using a cardboard snowflake template (see page 115), gently press an imprint into the center of each fondant round (see page 125).

8 Brush cakes with jam; top with fondant rounds. Blend luster with vodka, paint onto snowflakes; push silver cachous gently into rounds.

jewelettes

2 rings candied pineapple
3 whole candied apricots
1 cup pitted dried dates
⅔ cup red and green
    candied cherries
½ cup whole blanched almonds
1 cup brazil nuts
2 eggs
⅓ cup firmly packed
    brown sugar
1½ tablespoons dark rum
5 tablespoons butter, softened
¼ cup all-purpose flour
3 tablespoons self-rising flour

Topping

3 rings candied pineapple
½ cup red and green candied
    cherries, halved
½ cup brazil nuts
½ cup whole blanched almonds
⅓ cup apricot jam,
    warmed, strained

1 Preheat oven to 275°F.
Line 6-hole oversize (Texas) or
12-hole standard muffin pan
with paper baking cups.
2 Coarsely chop pineapple
and apricots, halve cherries and
nuts for large cakes. Chop fruit
and nuts slightly smaller for
small cakes.
3 Combine fruit and nuts in
medium bowl.
4 Beat eggs in small bowl with
electric mixer until thick and
creamy; add sugar, rum and
butter, beat until just combined.
5 Stir egg mixture into fruit
mixture with sifted flours. Divide
mixture among baking cups;
press firmly into baking cups.
6 Make topping; divide evenly
over cakes.
7 Bake large cakes about
1¼ hours, small cakes about
1 hour; cover cakes loosely with
foil halfway through baking time.
Cool cakes in pan.
8 Remove cakes from pan;
brush tops with jam.

Topping

Coarsely chop pineapple;
combine with remaining fruit and
nuts for large cakes. Chop fruit
and nuts slightly smaller for small
cakes. Combine fruit and nuts in
small bowl; mix well.

equipment

1. Piping bags
Available from cake decorating shops, chefs' supply shops and cookware shops, these are usually made from a waterproof material. Bags can also be made from wax or parchment paper; ideal for small amounts of icing (see page 117).

2. Rolling pins, brushes and metal spatulas
Mini rolling pins are available from cake decorating shops; fine artists' brushes from art supply stores, and metal spatulas from cookware shops.

3. Florist tape and wire
These are used to hold flowers and fondant shapes in position. Always cover wire or flower stems with florist tape if they are to be inserted into icing or cake.

4. Cutters
Come in all shapes and sizes; available from cake decorating or chefs' supply stores; these are usually made from metal or plastic.

5. Cake pans
Each recipe specifies the required muffin pan size – large, medium and small:
6-hole oversize (Texas) (¾ cup)
12-hole standard (⅓ cup)
12-hole mini (1½ tablespoons)

6. Paper and foil baking cups
Each recipe specifies the required paper baking-cup size, this denotes the pan size. Measured across the base:
oversize (Texas) muffin 2½ inches
freeform 2 inches
standard muffin 2 inches
mini muffin 1¼ inches
foil baking cups 1 inch

7. Luster and edible color
Is a powder available from cake decorating suppliers and craft shops in metallic shades, and is applied with a paintbrush. It is considered 'edible' in Europe and classified non-toxic for decoration only in Australia and the United States. Edible glitter is a non-metallic decoration for cakes.

8. Templates, lace and stamps
Templates and rubber stamps can be bought from cake decorating shops, craft shops and some stationers.

9. Colorings
Many types are available from cake decorating suppliers, craft shops and some supermarkets; all are concentrated. Use a minute amount of any type of coloring first to determine its strength.

Colorings are also available in liquid, gel, powder and paste forms.
Powdered are edible and are used when primary colors or black are needed.
Concentrated pastes are a little more expensive but are the easiest to use; are suitable for both pastel and stronger colors.

10. Flower making tools
A ball tool is used to shape petals and flowers; a frilling tool is used to shape lily petals; stamens are used for flower centers. These can all be bought from specialist cake decorating suppliers.

11. Icing tubes
Are made from metal or plastic, and can be bought from cake decorating suppliers, some craft shops, supermarkets and cookware shops.

Melting chocolate

Place coarsely chopped chocolate in small heatproof bowl, over small pot of simmering water; stir occasionally, until chocolate is melted. It is important that water not be allowed to come in contact with the chocolate, if it does the chocolate will seize. You can melt chocolate in a microwave oven; melt on medium (55%) about 1 minute, stirring twice during melting.

Making small chocolate curls

Using a sharp vegetable peeler, scrape along the side of a long piece of room-temperature eating-quality chocolate. Clean the peeler often so that the chocolate doesn't clog the surface of the blade.

Making chocolate curls using melon baller

Spread melted chocolate evenly and thinly onto a piece of marble, laminated board or flat baking sheet; let stand at room temperature until just set but not hard. Pull a melon baller over the surface of chocolate to make curls. We used these as gum nuts (see page 103).

Painting foil baking cups & leaves with chocolate

Use a fine clean, dry paintbrush. Paint melted chocolate thickly inside each foil case or onto one side of a clean freshly-picked leaf; leave to set at room temperature.

Finishing chocolate foil baking cups & leaves
Carefully peel back case or leaf from chocolate. These can be made ahead and stored in an airtight container at room temperature until required. If the weather is hot, keep them in the refrigerator.

Coloring white chocolate
Using a skewer, add a few drops of coloring (the amount depends on the intensity of the coloring) into melted white chocolate and stir with a clean dry spoon, until color is even. Too much coloring will cause chocolate to seize, that is, clump and turn an unappealing color.

Making a piping bag
Cut a 12-inch square of parchment or wax paper in half diagonally; hold apex of one triangle towards you. Twist first one point, then the other, into a cone shape. Bring three points together; secure the three points with a staple; repeat with other triangle. Sticky tape will hold a wax bag together, but not one made from parchment paper.

Piping chocolate
Place melted chocolate into paper piping bag. Snip end from bag. Cover a baking sheet with parchment paper, pipe desired shapes; leave to set at room temperature. Gently lift chocolate shapes from paper.

Making simple syrup

Always place sugar and water in recommended size heavy-based pot. To prevent crystallization or graininess, the sugar must be completely dissolved before the mixture boils. Stir constantly over medium to high heat to dissolve sugar. If sugar grains stick to the side of the pot, use a clean pastry brush dipped in water to brush down the sides of the pot.

Boiling simple syrup

After simple syrup comes to a boil, do not stir, and do not scrape pot or stir the syrup during cooking. Boil the syrup for about 5 minutes or until thick. Remove pot from heat; allow bubbles to subside before using. This stage can be measured accurately by buying a candy thermometer. The temperature should be 245°F. This stage is perfect for fluffy frosting.

Boiling simple syrup to hard crack

Bring sugar syrup to a boil, reduce heat; simmer uncovered, without stirring for about 10 minutes or until mixture is golden. Remove from heat; let stand until bubbles subside before using. If using a candy thermometer, mixture should be between 280°F and 310°F, depending on the color required. The longer the toffee boils and colors the harder it will set.

Candy thermometer

Thermometer should be stainless steel and have a clip to attach to the pot. Once sugar is dissolved, place thermometer in small pot of cold water (mercury must be covered). Bring the water to a boil, check thermometer for accuracy at boiling point. When simple syrup comes to a boil, place thermometer in syrup (mercury must be covered). Boil to the required temperature. Return thermometer to pot of boiling water, remove from heat, allow thermometer to cool in the water.

Checking toffee for hard crack

To test toffee for hard crack use a clean dry spoon and carefully drizzle some toffee into cold water. If it has reached hard crack it should set immediately. Always remove the pot from the heat and allow the bubbles to subside before testing.

Testing toffee

Remove set toffee from cold water and snap between fingers. It should be brittle and snap easily.

Making toffee shards

When toffee reaches a golden color, remove pot from heat, allow bubbles to subside; drizzle toffee from the back of a wooden spoon onto a parchment paper-lined baking sheet. Allow toffee to set at room temperature. Remove shards from paper using a spatula. Immediately position on cake.

Shaping toffee over rolling pin

When toffee reaches a golden color, remove pot from heat, allow bubbles to subside. Drizzle toffee from wooden spoon onto a rolling pin, covered with parchment paper. Allow toffee to set at room temperature. Slide parchment paper off rolling pin to remove toffee shapes. Immediately position on cake.

Fondant is a soft icing made from powdered sugar, gelatin, glucose and glycerine and it comes in two types: prepared fondant, which is used as a quick way to ice a cupcake, and modeling fondant (recipe page 75), which is used for making icing shapes. Both types can be bought ready-made from cake-decorating shops and some gourmet grocery stores.

Coloring prepared fondant

After kneading fondant until smooth, use a skewer to color fondant; kneading coloring into fondant until desired color is achieved. The amount of coloring needed will depend on the intensity of the coloring used.

Covering cakes with prepared almond paste or fondant

Brush cakes lightly and evenly with jam. Roll almond paste or fondant to desired thickness; lift onto cake with hands or rolling pin. Smooth surface with hands dusted with powdered sugar, ease paste or fondant around side and base of cake; trim excess with sharp knife.

Shaping flowers from modeling fondant

Cut out flowers using cutter of choice, place flower on clean folded dish towel. Using ball tool, gently shape flower; leave to dry.

Making butterfly from modeling fondant

Roll out fondant to ⅛-inch thickness. Cut out wings, place damp wire into each wing; dry flat. Make body of butterfly by molding a piece of fondant; attach wire to body.

  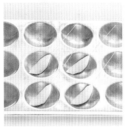 

Shaping butterfly
Bring wires, with wings attached, together. Use florist tape to secure wires and shape butterfly.

Making lily petals from modeling fondant
Knead fondant; roll to a thickness of ⅛ inch. Using the lily petal cutter, cut out 6 petals for each flower. Frill along each edge, using thicker edge of frilling tool. Gently score two lines on each petal.

Drying lily petals
Dry individual petals in round-based muffin pans or soup spoons. Bend the wire at a 90-degree angle from the petal.

Assembling lily
Wet one end of single wire lengths, insert into end of each petal; dry on parchment paper-lined tray. For flower center (pistle), roll tiny balls of fondant. Wet one end of single wire length, insert into balls; pinch balls several times with tweezers. To assemble lily, attach five stamens to pistle with florist tape. Attach one to two petals at a time, around pistle, using florist tape.

Piping choux pastry

Spoon choux pastry into piping bag fitted with a ½-inch plain tube. Hold piping bag vertical to parchment paper-lined baking sheet; quickly pivot wrist, piping tiny dollops (equal to ¼ teaspoon) of choux pastry ¾ inch apart, onto tray.

Piping meringue

Spoon meringue into piping bag fitted with a ½-inch plain tube. Hold piping bag vertical to the cake, piping a spiral from the outside to the center of the cake.

Piping lines with royal icing

Spoon icing into piping bag fitted with a small plain tube. Gently touch surface with tip of tube, lightly squeezing piping bag. As icing comes out, lift tube up from surface, squeezing to desired length. Stop squeezing bag, placing icing down onto surface. Even pressure is paramount – too much will give uneven thickness, too little pressure and the line will break.

Piping cornelli pattern with royal icing

Spoon icing into piping bag fitted with a small plain tube. Hold tube tip close to cake surface so that icing attaches without tube scraping cake or flattening the icing line. Pipe a continuous, meandering line of icing; move tip up, around and down to produce a lacy effect – don't let lines touch or cross.

Piping basket weave with royal icing

Using a basket weave tube, pipe a long vertical line from the top of the cake to the bottom, followed by short horizontal lines across the long vertical line. The horizontal lines should be a tube-width apart.

Pipe the next long vertical line at the end of the previous short horizontal lines.

Pipe short horizontal lines into the gaps, between the two vertical lines.

Repeat previous steps, continuing the basket weave design until the design meets with the starting point.

Using a serrated knife carefully shave edges of cake away.

Using a small clean paint brush, lightly and sparingly brush fruit individually with egg white; dip wet fruit in sugar. Place frosted fruit on parchment paper-lined tray. Leave about 1 hour or until sugar is dry.

The best results are achieved by using several doilies still joined together, pieces of plastic backed lace tablecloths or thick fabric lace, as they are easier to lift away from the cake once dusted with powdered sugar.

Place chocolate syrup into paper piping bag. Starting in the center of the cream topped cake, pipe a spiral. Using a skewer, gently drag through the spiral design, from the cake center to the edge of the paper case.

Drying pears and pineapple

Fruit needs to be sliced thinly and evenly – a mandoline or v-slicer is ideal, or use a very sharp knife. Using a clean pastry brush, brush both sides of sliced fruit with sugar syrup. Place fruit on wire rack over a baking sheet. Bake for specified time.

Shaping dried pears and pineapple

Dried fruit slices must be lifted from wire rack immediately after baking to prevent sticking. For pear slices, shape by pinching narrow end; dry on wire rack. For pineapple slices, pinch center of each slice; dry over egg carton.

Coloring sugar

Use granulated or superfine sugar, depending on the texture you prefer. Place required amount of sugar in a plastic bag, add a tiny amount of coloring; work coloring through sugar by 'massaging' plastic bag. Sugar will keep in a jar at room temperature indefinitely.

Marking fondant

Roll fondant to desired thickness; place textured templates onto fondant, pressing gently to leave an imprint. Lift template away from fondant. Or, gently press cardboard stencil into fondant, leaving imprint. Paint imprint with coloring or fill with colored sugar or sprinkles. Or, using a small, clean brush, paint design on stamp with colored paste; gently press stamp onto fondant, to leave a colored imprint.

glossary

after dinner mints mint squares coated in dark chocolate.

almonds

blanched brown skins removed.

meal also called ground almonds. You can make your own meal by grinding blanched almonds in a nut mill or food processor until they reach the consistency of cornmeal.

sliced paper-thin slices.

slivered small lengthwise-cut pieces.

brandy snap is a crisp, wafer-thin sweet cookie similar to ginger snaps.

buttermilk sold in the refrigerated dairy compartments in supermarkets. It is the liquid left after cream is separated from milk.

cachous small, round cake-decorating sweets available in silver, gold and various colors.

candied fruits fruits that have been cooked in heavy syrup.

chocolate

bars made of milk, white or dark compound chocolate; good for melting and molding.

dark we used premium-quality dark chocolate, not compound.

milk primarily for eating.

topping also called chocolate sauce.

white eating chocolate.

chocolate hazelnut spread also known as nutella.

cocoa powder also known as cocoa; dried, unsweetened, roasted ground cocoa beans.

coconut

flaked dried flaked coconut flesh.

liqueur we used malibu.

shredded thin strips of dried coconut flesh.

coffee-flavored liqueur we used either tia maria or kahlua.

cream cheese commonly known as philadelphia cream cheese, it is a soft cow-milk cheese with fat content of at least 33%.

eggs some recipes in this book call for raw or barely cooked eggs; exercise caution if there is a salmonella problem in your area.

Ferrero raffaello is a crispy, creamy almond and coconut bite-sized sweet.

flour, self-rising all purpose flour sifted with baking powder in the proportion of 1 cup flour to 2 teaspoons baking powder.

gelatin we used powdered gelatin as a setting agent.

ginger wine made with a grape base to which ginger, spices, herbs and fruits have been added.

hazelnut meal also called ground hazelnuts.

maple-flavored syrup made from sugar cane rather than maple-tree sap; used in cooking or as a topping but cannot be considered an exact substitute for pure maple syrup.

marmalade is a jam or conserve made with shredded citrus rind.

marsala a sweet fortified wine originally from Sicily.

mars bar a chocolate-coated caramel confectionery bar.

mascarpone a fresh, thick, triple-cream cheese with a delicately sweet, slightly sour taste.

milk we used whole homogenized milk.

mincemeat a sweet mixture of dried fruits, sugar, nuts and flavorings.

mixed dried fruit also known as dried fruit; commonly a combination of raisins, currants, mixed candied citrus peel and cherries.

peel also known as zest.

poppy seeds possessing a nutty, slightly sweet flavor and a dark blue-grey color, come from capsules inside an opium plant indigenous to the Mediterranean.

prepared fondant also known as soft icing and ready-to-roll.

rose petals, dried slightly chewy, dehydrated form of this popular flower. They can be used to flavor sweet and savory dishes.

rosewater extract made from crushed rose petals, called gulab in india; used for its aromatic quality in many desserts.

simple syrup a syrup made from equal parts sugar and water.

sugar

brown a soft, fine granulated sugar containing molasses to give its characteristic color.

powdered sugar also called confectioners' sugar; crushed granulated sugar with added cornstarch (about 3%).

pure powdered confectioners' sugar without the cornstarch.

vanilla sugar is granulated sugar flavored with a vanilla bean. Can be stored indefinitely.

vanilla

bean dried long, thin pod from a tropical golden orchid grown in central and South America and Tahiti. Tiny black seeds inside the bean are used to impart a vanilla flavor in baking and desserts.

extract distilled from the seeds of the vanilla pod.

vegetable oil any of a number of oils sourced from plants rather than animal fats.

conversion chart

measures

The difference between one country's measuring cups and another's is, at most, within a 2 or 3 teaspoon variance, and will not affect your cooking results.

All cup and spoon measurements are level. The most accurate way of measuring dry ingredients is to weigh them. When measuring liquids, use a clear glass or plastic jug with graduated markings.

We use large eggs with an average weight of 2oz.

dry measures

IMPERIAL	METRIC
½oz	15g
1oz	30g
2oz	60g
3oz	90g
4oz (¼lb)	125g
5oz	155g
6oz	185g
7oz	220g
8oz (½lb)	250g
9oz	280g
10oz	315g
11oz	345g
12oz (¾lb)	375g
13oz	410g
14oz	440g
15oz	470g
16oz (1lb)	500g
24oz (1½lb)	750g
32oz (2lb)	1kg

liquid measures

IMPERIAL	METRIC
1 fluid oz	30ml
2 fluid oz	60ml
3 fluid oz	100ml
4 fluid oz	125ml
5 fluid oz (¼ pint/1 gill)	150ml
6 fluid oz	190ml
8 fluid oz	250ml
16 fluid oz (1 pint)	500ml
1 quart	1000ml (1 litre)

length measures

IMPERIAL	METRIC
⅛in	3mm
¼in	6mm
½in	1cm
¾in	2cm
1in	2.5cm
2in	5cm
2½in	6cm
3in	8cm
4in	10cm
5in	13cm
6in	15cm
7in	18cm
8in	20cm
9in	23cm
10in	25cm
11in	28cm
12in (1ft)	30cm

Oven temperatures

These oven temperatures are only a guide for conventional ovens. For fan-forced ovens, check the manufacturer's manual.

	°C (CELSIUS)	°F (FAHRENHEIT)
Very slow	120	250
Slow	150	275-300
Moderately slow	160	325
Moderate	180	350-375
Moderately hot	200	400
Hot	220	425-450
Very hot	240	475

index